Your Connected Classroom

A Practical Guide for Teachers

Authored by

Kim Cofino
Chrissy Hellyer
Jeff Utecht

Contents

I. INTRODUCTIONS

Welcome! We're so glad you're here! We have been connecting our classrooms to the world for over fifteen years and the experience has been empowering, engaging, and enriching for our students, and for us as teachers! We have written this book for you, the classroom teacher, who are curious about creating a connected classroom and would like some practical advice for how to get started, why it's worth your time, and what you can expect once you get started.

Before we get into the nitty gritty of learning all about connected classrooms, we'd like to take a moment to quickly introduce ourselves. We are all experienced classroom teachers, having worked in several 1:1 schools, where our students were each provided a laptop. Not only have we all had the experience of connecting our classrooms to the wider world, but we all consider ourselves connected educators, with strong Personal Learning Networks that bring the world of education to us! Here's a little bit more about each of us, and why we're so excited to be sharing our connected classroom experiences with you:

Kim

I started my teaching career in Munich, Germany, where I was the only middle school technology teacher at Munich International School. I loved my job, but I felt really isolated. Although there were technology teachers in the upper and lower school, they didn't have exactly the same needs that I did as a middle school teacher (and they were both more experienced teachers than me, so at times I felt intimidated to ask questions). For my entire five years in Germany, the only professional development I had was an annual trip to a teacher's conference, and whatever came across my desk in the computer lab (this was about 20 years ago, so a shared book was pretty much the most I could hope for).

After my husband, Alex, and I, moved on to Kuala Lumpur, Malaysia in 2005, I happened to get a copy of Will Richardson's book, Blogs, Wikis, Podcasts and Other Powerful Web 2.0 Tools for the Classroom. That book inspired me to try some of these new web 2.0 tools with my students, and in order for me to feel prepared I started using them myself, as an educator.

Within one year, I had more professional connections than I had in the entire five years before. I felt like I was "in the loop" on everything related to educational technology since my professional development was on overdrive! In that one year, my students had participated in an award winning global project (thank you Clarence Fisher in Canada, Jabiz Raisdana in KL with me at the time, Lee Baber in the US, and Jamie Hide in Columbia, for collaborating with us), a number of smaller scale collaborations, and one long-term connection with my co-author, Chrissy Hellyer's, class in New Zealand.

And that was just the start of the amazing adventure of being a connected educator! Since then I've taught in three additional schools (in two more countries), developed my professional blog into a full time consulting career, started two educational technology related companies and one non-profit, and kept connected with my Personal Learning Network through it all. It's hard to believe that something as small as connecting your classroom can change your life, but it can. And that is why I'm so excited and passionate about sharing this adventure with you!

Chrissy

My teaching career began in Napier, New Zealand with a class of 34 Year 2 students and one (very old) desktop. When a new computer suite was built and an outside consultant began visiting our school once every three weeks, my students and I were "hooked!" Each week (on a Wednesday afternoon) we'd line up and head on over to the suite to work on our "projects" – we were actually building server-based portfolios of our learning!

Fast forward a few years later to a "semi-digital" classroom, 32 awesome Year 7s (Gr6), a digital weather station, a pod of 8 desktop computers, an interactive whiteboard, surround sound and ethernet access to the wider world (plus a computer suite to visit) and we REALLY thought we had it all! What started as a way to provide a window into the classroom for parents who couldn't make it into the classroom to see their children's learning (usually because of work commitments) became so much more. As we connected with our parent community an unexpected thing happened - we began to connect with the wider world in meaningful and authentic ways. Our enthusiasm grew with each connection we made. Once we had a class skype us to ask if the water swirled the opposite way when the toilet flushed! That sparked an awesome conversation about where in the world we were in relation to the USA and why they would think the water swirled the opposite way. Later that year our class connected with Kim Cofino's class in Kuala Lumpur, in what would become a long-term connection for both our classes and the start of an amazing professional and personal relationship for myself and Kim.

Several global collaborative projects later, a teacher exchange in Argentina, an interview in Bangkok and a few months after that, I found myself in a class of phenomenal 5th graders from all corners of the world and living in Bangkok, Thailand with the added bonus of working face to face with Kim and Jeff. When the opportunity to be the Elementary Technology and Learning Coach arose I spent a couple of years working with colleagues and their students. Time spent working with other schools and their teachers, as well as presenting and facilitating workshops grew during this time and after a year back in the classroom working with my favourite 3rd graders, I left the classroom again to move to Perth, Australia to begin planning learning experiences for teachers and students full time. In a few months the circle will be complete with a move back to my native New Zealand, albeit miles away from my home town and in the South Island. The great thing is no matter where we go our PLN comes with us and now you are a part of that PLN! Welcome!

Jeff

I began my career in the Elementary Classroom at a public school in Washington State. In 2001, I was the recipient of a Bill and Melinda Gates Grant called the Technology Leadership Program. With the first LCD projector in my school and 7 computers for my 34 students, this began my path into integrating technology into the classroom.

In 2002 my wife and I decided to move overseas to teach in International Schools. Over the next ten years we would move from Yanbu, Saudi Arabia where I helped to roll out a Palm Pilot Tungsten T5 one-to-one program to our seniors (the only one-to-one Palm Pilot program that I know of) to Shanghai, China where I helped to write and implement their one-to-one Macbook program for grades 6-12.

While in Shanghai I started my blog "The Thinking Stick" to share my passion for learning with the world. In 2007, I was invited to create an innovative conference focusing on learning and technology; the Learning 2.0 Conference (learning2.org) was initiated. My blog opened up my world and next thing I know I have authored chapters in numerous books, worked as the educational consultant for a wiki company, and began speaking at schools and educational events around the globe. I worked with politicians in Washington, DC and participated in The Educational Project at the invitation of the Prince of Bahrain. In 2008 my wife and I moved to Bangkok, Thailand where once again I helped to roll out their one-to-one program to students. In 2010 I was invited to present at the first TEDx conference in Bangkok.

As you read our bios you probably connected the dots to find where the overlap of the three of us began.- in Bangkok, Thailand at an International School.

The only problem is you'd be wrong. Our connection began long before we ever met face to face working at the same school. We first knew each other online through our connections and our connected classrooms. Kim and Jeff read and commented on each other's blogs. Chrissy and Kim worked on a virtual project together, and Chrissy followed Jeff on Twitter but he didn't follow her (a story she still loves to tell). This book is a culmination of our stories, our connections and our own learning as we have connected classrooms over the past 10 years.

Enjoy the journey!

II. NAVIGATING THIS BOOK

Now that you know a little bit about us, let's get back to the book. Although the focus of this book is on connecting your classroom, we believe you can do this best when you are a connected educator yourself. So, as you explore the summary descriptions of each chapter below, note that we're starting with connecting yourself, then connecting your classes to each other, next featuring some key elements of a connected classroom, and finally moving on to connecting your classroom to a wider audience. This happens to be the way we developed our own connected classrooms, which is why we recommend this progression to you. However, we know that everyone is on their own journey, so please, start with what feels right for you! We're here to support you in your adventure so don't be afraid to take risks and try new things! It's all worth it for the learning!

Additional Resources - Digital Content

This is not "just" a book. We have lots of additional resources to share with you, in particular digital resources that you can use with your students, additional website links for you to explore, and videos you can watch to go further in depth with the content.
To give you easy access to the digital content for this book, we're using something called QR codes.

Basically, a QR code is like a barcode that you would typically see in the grocery store, like this:

But a QR code is a little bit different because it can include even more data (that's why you see more than just straight lines in the QR code above). A QR code can take you to a website, it can automatically play a video, send a text, show you text. It can do lots of things! It's most popular use is as a paperless boarding pass for flights.

For our purposes in this book, we're going to include a QR code any time there is an external (digital) resource we are sharing with you.

To be able to read the QR code, you need a QR code reader for your smart phone. There are tons of options, and almost all of them are free.

Here are our favorites for iOS and Andriod:

 QR Reader for iPhone

 QR Code Reader (Android)

You can get these by going to the Apps store or the Play store and searching for QR code reader. They should be the first results and they should be free. Download them onto your phone, open the app, and point the camera at the QR code below and you'll automatically be taken to our resources page for this book!

This is the QR Code to access any content that is in blue type & underlined.

It will direct you to a page on our edurolearning.com website that is password-protected.

To access the content, use the password:

Edur0ycc

You'll notice when you visit the resource page that we have organized all of the downloads in one place to make it easy for you to access. They are organized according to each chapter, and we'll still include a QR code here in the book any time there is something you can download so you won't miss it!

Now you're all set to make the most of this book! You can read the book, and as you find QR codes, use your phone to scan the code to take you to directly to the resource or to our special resource page.

As you use QR codes throughout this book and think about how they can be used in your own classroom, understand that best case use for QR codes is to connect something in the physical world to something in the digital world. For example connecting digital resources to this physical book. QR codes can be used to connect physical objects in your classroom to digital resources you want students to access.

III. CHAPTER OVERVIEWS

CHAPTER 1: WHAT IS A CONNECTED CLASSROOM?

Understanding the essential elements of a connected classroom - one with just you and your students *and* one that is open to a wider audience - is the first step to connecting your classroom. This chapter will highlight the key pedagogies, including SAMR and TPACK, that will make your technology-rich classroom sound in learning principles, and share some key foundational elements about what makes a classroom connected, along with why that is so important in today's world.

CHAPTER 2: BECOMING A CONNECTED TEACHER

We feel the best way to truly understand a connected classroom is to connect yourself, as an educator first. This chapter shares the benefits of building a Personal Learning Network (PLN), and gives you all the tools you need to create one for yourself.

CHAPTER 3: CREATING A CONNECTED CLASSROOM

This chapter takes you step-by-step through the process of connecting your students to each other by creating a blended classroom. From the types of digital spaces you might use, to the people that need to be informed and engaged in the learning process (including parents and administrators), to our time-tested strategies for setting strong behavior expectations, this chapter has everything you need to get started connecting your classroom!

CHAPTER 4: MANAGING YOUR CONNECTED CLASSROOM

When every student has a device at their fingertips, classroom management can become even more stressful! But don't worry, we've got you covered in chapter 4! We discuss strategies for managing both behavior and the tools you'll use in your connected classroom. These are all of our favorite tips to make your technology-rich classroom a focused place of learning - not an opportunity for distraction!

CHAPTER 5: DESIGNING TECHNOLOGY-RICH LEARNING EXPERIENCES

Ensuring that the devices in your classroom are used purposefully, in order to enhance or transform learning, is a key component of a successful connected classroom. This chapter will walk you through how we design technology rich learning experiences that are authentic for students, include purposeful and focused use of technology, and put the student at the center in an inquiry-driven / project-based learning environment.

CHAPTER 6: MEDIA LITERACY IN YOUR CONNECTED CLASSROOM

As teachers, we are great at teaching literacy skills! But what are the key literacy skills in our digital world? How do we tell fact from fiction when it's all found at our fingertips from the results of a Google search? And beyond effective and critical searching skills, how do we ensure that our students are acting responsibly, safely and respectfully in digital spaces? Chapter 6 features a variety of essential lesson plans and skills that you can use with your students right away!

CHAPTER 7: TAKING YOUR CONNECTED CLASSROOM GLOBAL

Opening up your classroom to the world can be an intimidating thought. Chapter 7 walks you through all of the key elements to consider before you get started, and then provides a step-by-step guide to creating a custom collaboration that meets your curricular goals!

CHAPTER 8: HELPING PARENTS UNDERSTAND YOUR CONNECTED CLASSROOM

In addition to teaching our students how to be successful in the digital world, we need to help the parents of our students understand why this is so important. Being able to confidently and clearly discuss the rationale behind your connected classroom, as well as address very legitimate parent concerns is the focus of Chapter 8.

CHAPTER 9: CONTINUING THE LEARNING

We don't want this book to be the end of your journey! Chapter 9 highlights the most critical elements of this book and provides opportunities for you to continue your learning journey with us!

1 WHAT IS A CONNECTED CLASSROOM?

We all know technology has had a huge impact on our world, particularly in the last 20 years with the development of the internet. Now we can stay connected no matter where we are, as long as we have access to an internet connection. Plus, we have access to a never-ending supply of information, media, perspectives, and experiences right at our fingertips. This means we no longer need to be limited by the time and space of our traditional classroom structures. We can extend learning beyond classroom time, provide access to extensive resources and opportunities to discuss and reflect on those resources anytime and anywhere. At its essence, this is the foundation of a connected classroom.

For us, a connected classroom is making use of digital technologies to connect your students beyond the physical space (and time) limitations of the traditional classroom. Generally speaking, we call this a "blended classroom". Basically, this means making use of digital tools to allow learning to happen both within the traditional classroom setting, as well as beyond the limitations of physical space and time. A blended classroom can use any technology tool to connect students, share resources, provide forums for discussion, and opportunities for ongoing learning beyond the time and space of traditional lessons.

Using a standard blended classroom as a guide, we feel a connected classroom can be defined in two ways:

a blended classroom where the students are connected **to each other** (and their teacher) using a virtual classroom environment (like Google Classroom), and/or

a blended classroom where students (and their teacher) are connected to other students (and their teachers) in other classrooms **around the world.**

In both cases the use of digital technologies also allows parents, and sometimes (depending on sharing settings) other interested teachers and students, to have a window into classroom learning as well.

Let's dig a little deeper into these two definitions...

Connecting Your Students to Each Other

Usually, it feels most comfortable for teachers to connect their students to each other before connecting them to a wider audience, which makes a lot of sense! Figuring out the ins and outs of a blended learning environment can be complicated, especially if it's the first time you're connecting your class! We would like to give you a little bit of a preview here, and then go into the practicalities of actually setting this up in Chapter 3.

Connecting your students to each other means that you are providing a virtual space where all of your classroom resources, materials, assignments, discussions, and often times assessments, can be accessed. This is a huge advantage when you have a wide variety of digital resources, and allows you to easily empower your students to work at their own pace. This central space is the first place students would go for their next task, as well as the place they would "turn in" their finished work.

We'll be saying this again and again throughout the book, but it doesn't matter what tool you use, all that matters is that you have one place for students (and their parents) to go to access all of the digital resources for your class, and that the tool you chose at least meets the basic expectation of enabling you to provide a central resource sharing hub.

This kind of connected classroom is often private to just the students within your class (and their parents, if possible) and focuses highly on resource sharing and turning in assignments. Often times, you will also have students commenting on each other's work, discussing big ideas in forums, and exploring extension resources outside of class time. It's pretty much taking everything you do within the classroom and enabling it to happen anytime, anywhere.

To do this, you don't need much to get started. In fact, it doesn't matter if your students each have access to a device, or if they have to share, or you are using a computer lab. The idea is that the resources are available when needed, and that your students feel 100% comfortable accessing them whenever, wherever.

You can start connecting your students as soon as you have this virtual space set up. You'll want to introduce the idea to them during class time (and perhaps model the use of the site, if needed), and then kick things off as simply as posting a resource and asking students to comment for homework. Over time you'll start seeing the potential of the space for your students, and you may start adding more features that meet the needs of your individual students.

When you start connecting your students to each other, you are giving them an opportunity to learn about:

- Digital citizenship
- Copyright and Creative Commons
- Publishing content online
- Commenting and collaborating in digital spaces
- Time management and equitable access to resources

Whether you're keeping this space private to just you and your students, or if you're inviting parents in to have a look, it's always worth keeping the parents and your leadership team informed of what you're doing. You'll find sample permission slips in Chapter 3.

Connecting Your Students to the World

Once you have your students connected to each other, and you see how powerful anytime, anywhere learning can be, you might develop an interest in connecting your class to a wider audience. The big difference here is that often your virtual classroom space now needs to be public, so others can see and join in the conversation.

Connecting your classroom to the world takes a traditional blended classroom, as described above, and kicks it up a notch! Now your students can be collaborating with, learning from and creating content with students from other schools within your local region, and even globally! A globally connected classroom is one that empowers students to share their learning with a wider audience, that publishes their work in public spaces so others can see, comment and share, that utilizes a variety of tools (from creativity tools like WeVideo and iMovie, to social media tools like Twitter and Instagram, to communication tools like Skype and Google Hangout) to share and connect with others.

In Grade 3, Chrissy's students were studying Rocks & Minerals for Science. They were able to connect with an expert (a student's grandfather who was a retired geologist) via skype.

The student's fascination, focused attention and the learning facilitated by having a conversation with an actual geologist who showed them his tools was priceless. He shared what it was like to be a geologist and also showed the students some of his most memorable finds!

Use the QR code to read more …

Although there are many levels of a globally connected classroom, ultimately, a connected classroom is a learning environment that is open to the outside world. It's where students are engaged in real-life authentic learning starting in their own classroom and extends to reach other global learners.

Examples of how you can create a connected classroom include video conferencing applications, social media, and blogging. Start small! While it might sound daunting to connect your classroom to the outside world, there are a variety of small ways to make a big impact on your students' learning. Use an existing project to jump into a small, one-off, or simple global connection.

One way to do this is through video chat software such as Skype or Google Hangouts. There are many projects that already exist through these applications that you can tap into that will connect your classroom to another one around the globe.

This brings in many other elements to think about, which is why it is often best to start by simply connecting your students to each other. Connecting your classroom globally requires that you think about things like:

- Time zones
- Citation, copyright and sharing privileges and access
- Student authorship and voice in public spaces
- Building community in digital spaces
- Communicating across continents and cultures
- Sharing and collaborating in digital spaces
- Your school/district policy regarding use of student photo/videos

These can all seem like big hurdles before you start, but we promise the learning outcomes are worth it! The increased scope of learning, the harnessing of an authentic audience and the ability to share and get feedback on student work are just three of outcomes your students will experience when you take your classroom global! We'll share more about how to connect your classroom to the world in Chapter 8.

Keep in mind that whenever you take the leap into global collaboration, just like when you're connecting your students to each other, you'll want to ensure that your leadership team, and your students' parents are informed about what you're doing. You'll find sample permission slips in Chapter 3.

Common Pedagogies in a Connected Classroom

When we are connecting our students to each other, and beyond, we are truly redefining learning. We are doing things that were simply not possible without the technology we have today (and if they were possible, through opportunities like pen pals, they certainly weren't available with the speed, efficiency and reliability as they are today). When we think about all of the amazing learning opportunities a connected classroom provides, it's worth exploring the pedagogical foundations for making this shift.

All too often, teachers can get caught up in the excitement that technology provides, and end up using the tools just because they're there, rather than to enhance or transform learning. When you begin to connect your classroom, you want to make sure that the experiences you provide for your students are worth the time, energy and effort required to make them happen. We use two well-known, research-based methods for integrating technology into the classroom, SAMR and TPACK, to make these choices. Together, SAMR and TPACK work to provide a strong lens for you to evaluate the choices you make when you use technology.

Introducing SAMR

SAMR was developed by Dr. Ruben Puentedura, and is perhaps the most well-known and frequently implemented model of technology integration around the world. SAMR focuses exclusively on the way we use technology in the classroom, specifically on the level of impact the technology can have on learning.

SAMR stands for four levels of technology use:

Substitution: Technology acts as a direct tool substitute, no functional change.

Augmentation: Technology acts as a direct tool substitute, with functional improvement.

Modification: Technology allows for significant task redesign.

Redefinition: Technology allows for the creation of new tasks previously inconceivable.

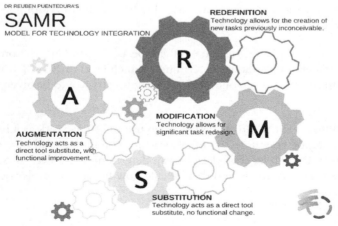

DR REUBEN PUENTEDURA'S

SAMR
MODEL FOR TECHNOLOGY INTEGRATION

REDEFINITION
Technology allows for the creation of new tasks previously inconceivable.

MODIFICATION
Technology allows for significant task redesign.

AUGMENTATION
Technology acts as a direct tool substitute, with functional improvement.

SUBSTITUTION
Technology acts as a direct tool substitute, no functional change.

Here's an example of progressing one specific task through the stages of SAMR. The purpose of this example is to demonstrate how one single task can be viewed through each level of SAMR.

> **Task: Write an essay which demonstrate your understanding of the environmental impact of plastics on the ocean.**
>
> **Substitution:** Use Google Docs to type your essay, print it out and hand it in to the teacher.
>
> **Augmentation:** Use Google Docs to type your essay, peer edit with a partner in the classroom, share with the teacher for feedback and assessment. Revise as needed until you have demonstrated mastery.
>
> **Modification:** Use Google Docs to collaborate with a student in another section of this class on a script for a mini video documentary about the environmental impact of plastics on the ocean.
>
> **Redefinition:** In collaboration with your partner in another section of this class, produce a video documentary about the environmental impact of plastics on the ocean. Use Google Docs to produce the script, your laptop/tablet to record clips, Creative Commons images and videos for clips that you can't take yourself, and YouTube editor to edit the video. Multimedia from both partners must be included in the final video, as well as an interview with an expert or experienced authority in the field.

As you can see, in the substitution and augmentation stage, the task remains the exactly the same: the final product is an essay. In the modification and redefinition stages, the task changes based on what is possible with the technology tools available. When we are talking about using technology to transform learning, we're talking about using technology in new and innovative ways, specifically those that were not possible before the development of the tools we have access to now.

Please note, in example above, you wouldn't be asking students to complete each stage, rather you would be determining which level of SAMR you will use to design the task - only one of these assignments would be given to the students.

The great thing about SAMR is that you can use the framework as a lens to view any (or all) of your assessment tasks. Once you understand how the progression from each level works, you can determine what level of SAMR your assessments currently are at, and then decide how far up the levels you would like to go.

One challenge with SAMR is that teachers often feel like it's a ladder they have to climb, that substitution is bad and redefinition is good. On top of that, there can be pressure to ensure that every single assessment or assignment should be at the redefinition level. However, we would advise against that kind of thinking. Not every lesson should be at the redefinition level, and there are plenty of times when substitution (or no technology at all) is the right tool for the task.

As you start to use the language of SAMR in your school community, you will find that it provides an excellent foundation for conversations about technology rich learning from staff meetings, to professional development, to team-level unit planning, to teacher observations. SAMR is an excellent reflective tool to ensure that your technology investment leads to transformational learning in purposeful, relevant and authentic classroom experiences.

Introduction to TPACK

TPACK takes a more holistic view of technology for learning. Instead of viewing technology use through the demonstration of learning, or the learning experiences, TPACK looks at the three critical domains of teaching within the whole structure of your lesson, unit, or academic year.

The three critical domains (of TPACK) are:

Technological Knowledge: what we know about technology

Pedagogical Knowledge: what we know about how people learn

Content Knowledge: what we know about our subject

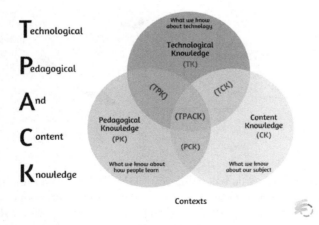

TPACK reminds us to strive for balance between all three of these domains, whether in a single lesson, a unit or a whole year of instructional practice.

As you are designing learning experiences, TPACK asks you to think about the time you spend in each domain, as well as the priority you put on each domain, to ensure that you are operating in the "sweet spot" of balance at the middle.

As educators we know that at times in our teaching, content is new and important and may take more of the focus, other times we want students to be able to demonstrate their learning in new and unique ways so technology skills may be the priority, other times we see that students may have struggled with content so we hone in on our pedagogical approaches. TPACK reminds us to work towards balance, while recognizing that there are times and phases when one might take priority over the others.

An example with TPACK could be:

You are teaching persuasive writing. You usually have students write an essay on the topic of their choice to the audience of their choice. Because students already are confident with the skill of actually getting their words to paper (through typing or handwriting), you don't need to spend any class time teaching them how to do that. Instead, you spend the majority of your time on the content area of persuasive language. In order to best support your students, you implement a variety of pedagogical approaches to ensure they understand persuasive language.

In terms of TPACK, this might look like this

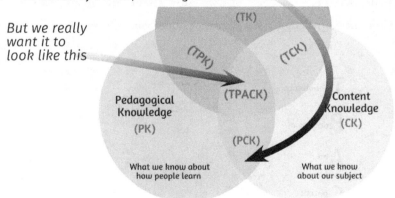

If you are working towards balancing your TPACK levels, you might think about re-evaluating this unit. Instead of having students write an essay, which they have done many times before, you might ask them to create a different product, one that uses elements of Modification and/or Redefinition from SAMR.

In this case, your unit might look like:

You are teaching persuasive writing. You have asked students to create a multimedia piece on the topic of their choice. This piece will be published online (this could simply be shared with parents, a specific audience that perhaps "needs persuasion", or the actual multimedia piece could created be in collaboration with another class somewhere else in the world). Because students may not have experience with the multimedia tools needed to successfully create this product, you are spending a specific chunk of class time facilitating their learning of these tools. This could be done with peer-experts, sandbox exploration time, the use of tutorials, or whatever way makes the most sense for you. Of course, you also need to focus on the skill of persuasive writing, and the pedagogical approaches that best meet the needs of your students.

In terms of TPACK, this might look like this:

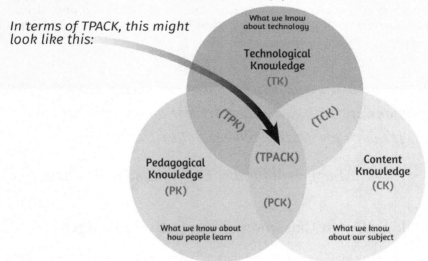

As you can see, SAMR fits right into TPACK, in helping you evaluate your use of technology when you recognize if certain elements are out of balance.

Many teachers like TPACK because of its holistic perspective. It can feel more approachable, especially to teachers who prefer "big picture" thinking, or are not yet ready to address specific units or lessons.

A challenge with TPACK is that it is so general, and does not provide a framework for understanding truly transformational learning with technology. As we explored above, this is where SAMR comes in. The Technological Knowledge portion of TPACK can be merged with SAMR so that the two models can be used together.

It's important to note that neither of these models are making a value statement on how, when, why or where you use technology in the classroom. Rather they are asking you to be a reflective practitioner and reflect on potential opportunities for transformative learning, which balance your use of technology with the other critical domains of teaching (pedagogy and content).

Why should our classrooms be connected?

Now that you have a deeper understanding of the two types of connected classrooms, as well as the pedagogical foundations for both, you might be wondering - is it worth it? It's important to understand that connecting your classroom can be a lot of work, particularly the first time around, and we want to make sure that the results of your time and energy truly do transform learning.

Connecting your students with others around the globe helps your students break down the walls that traditionally exist in the classroom to build bridges to other people, countries, and cultures.

When we listen with less judgment, we always develop better relationships with each other. It's not differences that divide us. It's our judgments about each other that do.

Margaret Wheatley in "Willing to be Disturbed"

Breaking Down Classroom Walls to Build Bridges

Walls are going up. Lines are being drawn. Countries are polarized by politics. It's time we as educators take a stand for the future generations and expect our students to listen and act with empathy. And to do that, they need it modelled and taught to them. Did you know that research shows that learning another language improves tolerance? To learn another language, one must take risks and acknowledge that his/her lens isn't the only lens to view the world. This opens the door for empathy and tolerance.

When we begin to see life through others' eyes, we have taken a step forward in unifying as a global society. In "How Learning a New Language Improves Tolerance", author Amy Thompson states,

Cultural competency is key to thriving in our increasingly globalized world.

This article, <u>Teaching Strategies: The Importance of Empathy</u> has even more ways to encourage empathy in the classroom. By flattening our classroom walls, we can literally offer the world to our students! They can experience life like never before.

So how do we do this in the classroom? One way to encourage is to connect your class to other classes from around the world.

This is the QR Code to access
any content that is in blue type
& underlined.

It will direct you to a page on
our edurolearning.com website
that is password-protected.

To access the content,
use the password:

Edur0ycc

2 BECOMING A CONNECTED TEACHER

Using technology to connect your students to others around the globe helps your students break down the walls that traditionally exist in the classroom to build bridges to other people, countries, and cultures. When teaching your students how to think globally and connect with others around the world, it's important that you do the same.

We know this book is about connecting your classroom, but we really do believe that you can do this best (and easiest) if you are a connected teacher first! Truly, the best way to understand the power of global connections for your students is to be connected yourself.

We can all relate to the feeling of being isolated in our professional practice. Whether we are the only teacher of a certain subject in a grade level, or if our colleagues are at a different point in their professional journey then we are, or if we're simply physically isolated due to our school location or structure, it can be hard to find exactly *what* you need for professional development, exactly *when* you need it.

That's exactly what a Personal Learning Network will provide: just in time learning, customized just for you!

Building a personal learning network (PLN) can help you get the most out of your time online. Rather than searching blindly for topics that you teach, you can make a curated list of educators to follow. Developing your own personal learning network will help you not only understand some of the tools, but it will give you a good idea of the value of the learning experience, the logistics and the challenges your students might experience. Of course, you don't have to know all the details about all the tools, but just going through the experience yourself may help you feel more confident when you start to explore with your students.

Communities vs Networks

To get us started, let's define the difference between a community and a network - since you'll be tapping into a variety of communities to build your customized network.

Communities

Communities are nothing new to humans. We have been creating them since the beginning of time. Merriam-Webster Online defines community as "an interacting population of various kinds of individuals". The neighborhood in which you live is one example of a community. You have a common interest of living in the same area as your neighbors. You might not know all of them, or even like all of them, but you belong to a group of people with a common interest, in this case, location.

The same applies to communities on the Internet. Using one of the largest online communities, Facebook, as an example, we can see how online communities are developed. There are over 2 billion users on Facebook; they are a community of users who have joined that site, created profiles, uploaded pictures, and communicate regularly with people they know. As a user of Facebook, you become a part of that community. You have a common interest in connecting with other people you know, or connecting with others that share a common personal or professional interest. Once you create an account, you are welcomed into the Facebook community. What you do and how involved you are once you get there is up to you.

Networks

Once you join a community, you can create a network within it that will serve your purpose. Merriam-Webster Online gives a definition of networks as being "a usually informally interconnected group or association of persons".

This is the type of network the Internet allows. Once you join a community you then create your network within it by reaching out and connecting with others. Facebook works on this principle. Joining the community of Facebook gives you nothing. Creating a network of friends and family is the power that lies within the Facebook community. You will never know the billions of members in the community called Facebook. You won't interact with most of them. Much like the neighborhood you live in, or the grocery store you shop at, they are there going about their daily lives in your community and you within theirs. But within that community you have the potential to find people you care about, people you can learn from, and friends you enjoy being around. Facebook is the community that allows the connections to happen between community members to form networks.

Creating Your Personal Learning Network

Now that we have defined the difference between a community and a network you can start thinking about which tools make the most sense for you to use. We're going to share some of our favorites here, feel free to test them all out and see what suits you the best.

Tool 1: Twitter

Twitter is probably our favorite tool - and the one where you will likely find the most educators. This makes it an amazing space, but also an overwhelming space. We're going to take a deep dive into Twitter here because we think you'll get the most bang for your buck with this tool, but don't worry there are some more options within this section too!

To get started with Twitter, you'll need to create an account at Twitter.com. This allows you to join the community of millions of educators who are sharing and exploring new ways of learning. However, just like in Facebook, joining Twitter, becoming part of the community is just the first step. Creating your personal network within Twitter is where the power lies in these digital spaces.

Twitter is a great social network to use to build your PLN. You can follow a community by following an education based hashtag, or you can follow educators directly. There are many Twitter lists that exist that contain educators you can follow based upon grade, subject, or location where you teach. These lists will give you a starting point of who to follow

While it may be tempting to just have someone tell you who to follow, it's important to spend the time to curate your network so you're getting value from it. Follow educators that you aspire to be like, that have innovative ideas you'd like to try, or that are in the same state or country as you. Start off small – it's better to have a few quality educators in your list that you can follow, rather than be overwhelmed with a large list.

The Parts of a Tweet

Name of Twitter user and their handle

hashtag

URL to content

Message

Like it so you can find it later

Reply to this user

ReTweet and share with people that follow you

The parts of a tweet image shows you the different parts of a tweet. Twitter uses many of the same functions as other social networks.

@ - identifies a user and is how you reply to them. So if you wanted to include/reply/tag Jeff in your tweet, you would add @jutecht, or to include/reply/tag Kim add @mscofino, or to include/reply/tag Chrissy add @nzchrissy. Or you can click on the reply button found on a tweet.

RT - This is unique to Twitter and is a retweet. In other words, you like what someone shared and you think the people that follow you would like it as well so you want to share it or "retweet" it to them so they too see this amazing resource you found. It's how resources get shared on Twitter between different users and communities.

- The hashtag tells you what community this resource was shared with. In the example above the tweet was shared with the #gegwa community, the Google Education Group in Washington State.

Goo.gl - This is known as a URL shortener. You will see them in different formats. Bit.ly and to.co are other URL shorteners that you will see often. They take long URLs and shortened to save space. These lead you to websites and resources shared in the tweet. In other words...the good stuff!

The Hashtag

The # symbol is not the number symbol anymore, in today's connected world it's a hashtag. The hashtag was first used on the Internet on Twitter in August 2007 (Hashtag.org, 2013). The tweet reads as follows:

> ?how do you feel about using # (pound) for groups. As in #barcamp [msg]??

Twitter was the first place hashtags were used in Social Media and from there, they quickly become the foundation of the way people on Twitter communicated to find each other and to create ... you guessed it ... communities. Twitter adopted the hashtag and soon made it an active link searchable by everyone on Twitter to find each other.

Now we can use hashtags to find and build the communities we want to belong to and after add the people we want to follow.

Searching for your community

Lucky for us some educators have taken it upon themselves to create easy-to-search websites of educational hashtags. Our (old school) favorite is Cybrary Man's Educational Hashtag Database. It might not be the prettiest of web pages, but it is a great list of educational Twitter communities that exist on Twitter. Shake Up Learning also has a nice database of educational Twitter communities. You can visit them both and decide for yourself which one works best for you.

Understanding how to get these hashtags to starting to build your PLN is better explained in a video.

Using the QR Code below, watch the video to see how to start building your PLN by finding the educational communities that already exist on Twitter

Communities as Twitter lists

Another feature of Twitter to help you build your PLN is the ability to create lists of users. Basically, you get to create your own "community list" based on whatever criteria you see fit. It could be topic based, location based, or passion based. You get to decide. Twitter lists can be either private or public and public lists are great, as they allow others to share their lists with you so you can follow them.

On the next page are some lists worth taking a look at. These are just suggestions, please do not follow them all. Instead, take some time to scroll through, see if that list will add value to your network and then and only then do you subscribe to the list and follow the people within it. You can even subscribe to a list without following all of the users in the list, or just subscribe to some of the users within a list. Scrolling through the lists of other Twitter users you learn from is a great way to pick and choose new people to follow to add to your network.

Twitter Lists:

COETAILers: A list of international educators working at international schools in foreign countries.

Midwest Educators: A list of educators in the Midwest United States

State by State list of educators to follow: Keith O'Neal has created a list for every state in America. Take some time to browse all the lists that he has created and subscribe to the ones you want to follow.

Twitter Lists - Three Perspectives

We all love Twitter lists! Have a look at how we've used them to create communities within our Twitter PLNs!

Chrissy's Lists of Educators

I was always looking for global partners for collaboration projects so it made sense to begin grouping my PLN by location. In the end though, it didn't really matter where you were, we made it work!

- *Educators in Asia*
- *Worldwide Educators*
- *Kiwis & Aussies (New Zealand & Australia Educators)*
- *International Educators*

Jeff's list of Pacific Northwest Educators.

I wanted to connect with a personal community of educators using Twitter in the states of Washington, Oregon, and Idaho. Now when I need to find a teacher to connect too around a topic that might include something in the Northwest, say Salmon, Volcanos, earthquakes or the Oregon Trail, I have my community here that I can tap into. I have educators that I can reach out to help connect my class "beyond the walls" of the classroom.

*When you click on the Pacific Northwest Educators link you will be taken to my list, where you can have a quick browse to see if these are educators you might want to be part of your PLN. If so click on the **subscribe** buttons on the left and that list will be added to your twitter account. By finding a list, much like finding your hashtag communities, you instantly get to create a network of people to follow.*

Managing your PLN

Now that you have those two different ways of finding your communities on Twitter. It's time to learn how to manage all this new and exciting information coming at you. There are many different tools to manage your PLN.

One of our favorite social media management tools is Hootsuite.

If you'd like to give it a try, check out this video from Jeff. He shares his personal setup of Hootsuite.

The video includes step-by-step instructions of how to set up your own Hootsuite account so that you can start to manage the information coming at you so you don't feel overwhelmed!

Tool 2: Social Networks (Like G+ and Facebook)

You may have heard of Google+ you may even have an account. But chances are, you might not be aware of the amazing amount of educational (and specifically edtech) communities within Google+.

These communities and networks can help you make the transition to being a connected teacher and having a connected classroom a smooth one. They are designed to allow you to share your experiences, ask for advice, and get inspiration for ways to bring technology into your classroom.

Some suggested circles:

- Connected Classrooms on G+
- Mystery Hangouts for Foreign Language Teachers
- Google Apps Educators
- Technology in Education

Tool 3: A News Reader (like Flipboard or Netvibes)

Once you start discovering educators in Twitter and social networks like Google+, you might notice that they are often sharing blog posts. You can keep up with the blogs that you find especially interesting or insightful using a news reader like Flipboard or Netvibes.

When you've set it up, your news reader will aggregate all of the new posts on those fantastic blogs in one place – like an e-mail inbox for websites and blogs. Instead of scrambling around trying to find all the best new posts, just sit back and let them come to you!

Tool 4: Podcasts

There are a number of educators who create podcasts. These are basically like radio shows that you can subscribe to and listen to anytime.

Tool 5: VOIP (like Google Hangouts or Skype)

There are many free, web-based tools to help you connect with your PLN through video or audio chatting. Many expats already take advantage of the free, and very easy to use VoIP provider, Skype, but there are many more ways to connect to your network.

Google Hangouts can be used for chat conversations or video calls. You can make phone calls using wi-fi or data and send text message with your Google Voice or Project Fi phone number. Hangouts sync automatically across devices. If you start a Hangout on your computer, you can continue your chat on another device, like your phone.

Services like FlashMeeting, WizIQ and Elluminate also offer comprehensive options for teaching and learning together – with your PLN, and potentially with your classes.

Tool 6: Online Conferences (For Free!)

Over the past few years, more and more conferences have started offering unrestricted content from physical conferences online, using web 2.0 tools, and even hosting conferences entirely online. These conferences utilize social networks like Ning, blogs, wikis, podcasts, and vodcasts as a format for presenters to share their work.

Instead of requiring attendees to physically fly to a central location, all presentations are posted in a central place – available anytime, anywhere – for free! Not only is this a great way to learn about new techniques for your 21st century classroom, but you can also see a wide variety of web 2.0 tools in practice.

Become a Blogger (and a Twitterer)

Once you've gotten an idea of the web 2.0 world in education, you may want to add your voice to the mix. Everyone has something different to offer and there is an audience for every author in the demographic "Long Tail" of global education. In order to really bring your network together, you will need to share your own thoughts and learnings with your PLN.

Blogs and Twitter go hand in hand. A blog is the perfect space for thoughtful reflection, a place to connect your learning and create something new. Twitter is a powerful tool for sharing quick snippets of your thinking, for connecting with others, and for widening your information consumption a little bit at a time.

Embracing the power of web 2.0 is as simple as having an open mind and a sense of adventure. There is more to see, hear and experience than one person could ever consume. Take a look around, you're guaranteed to find exactly what you need, right when you need it!

Here are some of Kim's blog posts about this topic:

- First Steps Toward Becoming a 21st Century Educator
- How to Connect Your Students Globally
- 5 Tips for Creating a Global Classroom
- Making the Connection
- The Power of Audience

And some personal reflections/experiences that might help demonstrate the value of having these connections:

- Sunday 2.0: An Average Sunday in a Web 2.0 World
- Two Crises: Many Connections

Growing Your PLN

How fast you grow your network is completely up to you. We have found there is a tipping point around 50 people. Most educators all of a sudden start to see the value of a PLN once they have around 50 people in their network. Grow your list by looking at what others are sharing. If you find you continually find yourself reading tweets from a specific person, that is a good person to follow. Maybe you click on a link in a tweet or G+ post and find that perfect resource. Chances are that person will share other things you will find valuable in the future so follow them as well.

Once you have connected yourself and built your own personal learning network, you will have all the skills (and all the support) you need to successfully connect your class! We're going to start with connecting your students to each other in Chapters 3 - 5, and then go global in Chapter 6.

This is the QR Code to access any content that is in blue type & underlined.

It will direct you to a page on our edurolearning.com website that is password-protected.

To access the content, use the password: **Edur0ycc**

3 CREATING YOUR CONNECTED CLASSROOM

After developing your Personal Learning Network, and starting to see the power of connected learning, we hope you're ready to start connecting your students (or maybe you skipped that chapter, and you're just ready to start connecting your class)! Either way, let's get started!

Step 0: Informing Your Leadership

We've mentioned it a few times above, but before you get started creating your connected classroom, especially if this is not part of your school culture, it's a good idea to at the very least, inform your divisional leadership of your plans

You'll want to highlight:

- What you plan to do with your students
- How this enhances or transforms learning
- What students will learn in addition to the content you are able to teach in traditional methods
- How you plan to keep parents informed
- An opportunity for your leadership to come by and see the learning in action

All of the administrators we've worked with have been enthusiastic about connected learning - if not immediately, then definitely after we've explained the clear value and purpose behind the use of technology. It's important to have those clearly articulated so you can help both your administrators, and the parents of your students (see step 2), understand the value of connecting your class.

Step 1: Creating Your Virtual Classroom

To create your connected classroom, all you need to do to get started is to create a virtual classroom space online. As we said before, it doesn't matter what tool you use, you just want to create that central digital version of your classroom, online. This is a space where you will share resources, post assignments, engage students in learning opportunities outside of class time, highlight great student work, and link to the online spaces where your students are sharing.

To get a preview of what that might look like, here are some great examples:

- PageZ (Zoe Page) : Grade 1, Yokohama International School, Japan
- Peeking into Division 16 (Karen Lirenman, shared by Tammy Dewar) : 5, 6, 7, 8 year olds, Canada
- Learning in 21 (Robin Sully) : grade 3 & 4, Canada
- IFTS Central Coast (Dean Groom) : Grade 7 / 8, Australia
- Ms. Madrid (Rebekah Madrid) : Secondary Humanities, Yokohama International School, Japan
- Melville Room 8 (Stephanie Thompson) : Middle School, currently in Singapore
- On an e-Journey with Generation Y (Anne Mirtschin): Secondary, Australia
- KnightsRok (Liz Cho) : Teacher collaborative blog, South Korea

You can see in all of these examples that the core of the connected classroom is a home base. This is the one central space where all your resources are linked, where students can find what they need, and contribute what's expected of them.

Bonus! Check out
Eduro Learning's video:

Top 10 Tips for the
Connected Classroom

As we've mentioned a number of times, it really doesn't matter what tool you use, as long as it provides a few specific options:

- The ability to link to other things on the internet.
- The ability to choose when you want to share things publicly or privately (or, if needed, to make the entire space private).
- The ability to customize the space enough so that both you and your students can easily find what you're looking for.
- Automatic archive of resources, posts, and student learning over time. You may want to use this same space again next year and it's great to be able to look back at what you did in previous years. This also makes it super easy to support absent students and to track (and remember) what you've done in each class.

A few things that are nice to have, but could be integrated by mixing and matching some other tools:

- A place for forum discussions and/or comments - note that often forum discussions allow for threaded conversations and comments sometimes do not.
- To be able to mix and match public and private spaces (although you can easily do this by using a variety of tools linked to your home base). It's great to have the ability to create a specific space for sharing with a wider audience - to prepare you and your students for global collaborations (you'll read more about this in Chapter 7).
- A calendar to post assignment deadlines.
- An "About Me" page introducing you (it's amazing how much students love to read this - and so do their parents!)
- An "About Us" page introducing your class.
- An easy way for parents to "subscribe" to updates from your page
- An opportunity to embed social media tools like Instagram, Twitter, Facebook or Flipboard.
- A way to track visitors to your site - either with a public map or stats that only you can see. This can be highly motivating for both teachers and students!

Within your home base space, you might choose to include:

- extension resources
- artifacts that recap the learning of the day - from pictures of whiteboard notes to videos from the class to student-authored collaborative notes
- screencasts & how to videos
- opportunities for focused & extended discussion
- opportunities to highlight great work completed by students

- opportunities to promote key learning from other students
- opportunities to model sharing your thinking in online spaces

If possible, it's great to also provide some student ownership of your home base, this could be:

- student-authored posts, notes, lesson recap, interesting connections
- links to student blogs, work, samples
- student-created guidelines to how we communicate, share and create in our blended learning environment.

Some popular tools (as of the writing of this book) for creating a home base are:

- Google Classroom
- Google Blogspot
- WordPress Blogs
- SeeSaw (particularly for Elementary Schools)
- Weebly
- Wix

Case Study:
http://kimcofino.com/blog/2011/10/09/mix-and-match/

It's hard to believe that it's only been a year since we started using Google Apps for Education at YIS! Around this time last year we were still using FirstClass and just about to make the transition to Google, mainly for e-mail purposes, but in that time we've started to develop some great ideas for more efficiently communicating and collaborating with students, parents and teachers.

Along with Google Apps, this is the first year (starting in August) that we've required all teachers to have a blog on The Learning Hub (our school blogging portal). The previous two years have been voluntary, to give teachers a time to explore and see what works. Fortunately, we have a very enthusiastic staff, and they've seen lots of great opportunities for utilizing the blogs as a communication and learning portal for parents and students. By this time next year, we'll be working towards blogs as e-portfolios for students, on the same platform.

Combining our use of Google Apps and our WordPress blogs on The Learning Hub has really started to create a dynamic and practical blended learning environment for our school community. Although I'm sure we still have lots of opportunity for growth, I'm really proud of what we've started to implement already: (Read more by accessing our digital content QR Code)

Step 2: Informing Parents

Now that you have your home base, it's time to let parents know what's happening. You'll want to share your learning goals with the parents of your students, as well as the structure for how you hope to achieve those goals. Because many parents may not have experienced this kind of learning when they went to school it's very important to make sure they understand both what you're doing and why you're doing it (particularly in terms of the learning outcomes). It's important to note that parents just want the best for their children, so making sure to address and identify some of their concerns at the outset will go a long way towards securing their support. Some things you might want to mention:

- Learning is the priority - students will still learn the key content (like writing, or speaking, or reading) that they always learned. It's not all about the tech (and they certainly might not be as excited about the tech you plan to use as you or your students might be).

- This is a great opportunity to teach online safety and responsibility (often called digital citizenship), which is key skill for our hyper connected world - and one that is often neglected because we assume that "kids already know it".

- You are creating classroom guidelines for behavior in this space with your students, to ensure that student safety is prioritized. Although you can't watch everything, every minute of the day, you are taking proactive action to ensure that students are not bullied, bullying others, exposed to explicit information, or harassed by strangers.

- Although you're going to be using technology in new ways, you are prioritizing balance - for example: we still read paper books, we still spend time outside, and we still talk to each other.

Along these lines, we always recommend highlighting the positive and assuming that parents would like their children to be involved in such a great learning experience. This helps set a positive tone for your connected classroom with your entire classroom community.

Because every school has different structures in place, we've tried to provide a variety of examples that you can build from in developing informational resources for parents. Feel free to edit, adapt and revise all of these examples so that they best fit your school context.

Essential Documents for the Connected Classroom

As we know, every school is different, and of course, every school is in a different place regarding its use of technology. Therefore some documentation that might be readily available in one school might be non-existent in another school. So, we have provided a range of documents that you can tailor to your needs - from the school that has no documentation at all, to the school that already has a strong Responsible Use Agreement in place. We've organized the resources by the amount of documentation available to the teacher so you can find the best starting point for your situation.

Little to No Documentation Available at Your School

If you're in a school where sharing learning online, particularly in public spaces, is rare, and you don't already have existing documentation to work with, this is a good place to start. You'll note that these documents may be about specific kinds of projects (like blogging) and you will need to tailor them specifically to the work you're doing with your students.

Permission Slip

After you've informed your school administrator and anyone else in your school who needs to know about your new project, the most important element is to let parents know what you're planning. Before beginning any global collaboration, or sharing student learning in public online spaces, we recommend sending home a permission slip to inform parents.

A successful permission slip will:

- present your project idea in a clear and organized way
- include the learning outcomes or goals for this project
- give educational context
- Include an explanation of how the project will work
- clearly articulate the purpose for the online component of learning
- be positive and enthusiastic about the learning opportunities for students
- make it easier for students to participate than for parents to "opt out"

You may need to create several permission slips over the course of one school year if you plan to do a variety of projects. Or you may choose to create one permission slip at the beginning of the year that covers many different forms of digital learning.

Sample Permission Slip: Blogging

> Page 3 of PDF:
> **Essential Documents for the Connected Classroom**
>
> To access the content, use the password: **Edur0ycc**

Additional Resources

- http://www.teachingsagittarian.com/technologycoach/blogging-contract/
- Blogging is Elementary: this blog post by Kim will give you an overview of how this unit was introduced to students
- Student Blogging Guidelines: this blog post by Kim shares student-created blogging guidelines that may be a good starting point for your class
- Connected Students through Blogging: this blog post by Chrissy that shares ten tips that may help get blogging starting in your classroom and keep it sustainable throughout the year.

Sample Permission Slip: Equipment Loan

If you are in an environment where there is limited access to devices, from laptops to iPads to Kindles, you might be interested in loaning them out to your students while they work on projects. This sample permission slip was created for a library with a selection of iPods to loan out, but can be easily adapted to just about any resource.

> Page 6 of PDF:
> **Essential Documents for the Connected Classroom**
>
> To access the content, use the password: **Edur0ycc**

Additional Resources

- iPod Learner's Permit: this blog post by Kim will provide some background on how we used the iPods within a library context

Some Documentation Available at Your School

If you're in a school where sharing online does happen, but it's not consistent, you may wish to create a Acceptable Use Policy for your students, and send it home to parents before starting your project. An AUP states that students will be using a variety of tools for multiple purposes and this single document is permission for any and all use of digital tools throughout the year. AUPs are used with both school-owned equipment, and can be applied to student-owned equipment during school hours.

A successful Acceptable Use Policy:

- clarifies expectations for behavior as well as technical use
- outlines the technology or tools available to students
- empowers students to make good choices
- describes outcomes if expectations are not met

Sample Acceptable Use Policy

Page 8-9 of PDF:
Essential Documents for the Connected Classroom

To access the content, use the password: **Edur0ycc**

Extensive Documentation Available at Your School

If technology is as "ubiquitous as air" in your school, you will probably find that there is a variety of documentation available for you to use. You might also be in the situation that your school automatically sends home documentation when students register so that there's really nothing you need to do to ensure that parents are informed about the online learning that's happening, or so that students are aware of the expectations.

However, it's always a good idea to go over the standard expectations that are consistent across the school, as well as identify elements that you, along with your students, feel are critical in your classroom. It's also worth reviewing the documentation available at your school so that you, as a teacher, are comfortable with the expectations. You might also notice that although documentation is readily available it may not be of high quality or cover all of the elements that are essential to you. In this case, you can always add additional elements specific for your classroom.

Sample Responsible Use Agreement

Page 11-19 of PDF:
**Essential Documents for
the Connected Classroom**

To access the content, use the
password: **Edur0ycc**

In the interest of comparison, we are providing a very thorough Responsible Use Agreement for you to explore so that you can see if your school includes all the necessary elements. If not, please feel free to adapt and revise to include the elements you need. This document was developed by all stakeholders at Yokohama International School, Japan, while Kim was facilitating the implementation of the Connected Learning Community (1:1 Program). It is worth noting that many schools have changed the language to be Empowered Use Agreement (rather than Responsible Use Agreement). Feel free to adjust the language to best suit your needs.

Step 3: Setting Behavior Expectations

One of the great benefits of creating a connected classroom is the opportunity to teach students about digital citizenship, specifically student safety and responsibility. You'll want to make sure that the conversations that happen in this digital space reflect the values and behaviors that you would see in your physical classroom as well. We'll have more on this in Chapter 5, but this section is designed to give you a bit of a preview.

As you're embarking on this digital adventure with your students, we believe it's also critical to develop shared expectations for behavior in these spaces. Of course, you'll want to parallel the expectations from your physical classroom into the digital classroom, but especially if this experience is new for you or your students, we recommend that you are very explicit about defining those boundaries.

All of us have worked with students, either within our classes, or in supporting other teachers as learning coaches, to help them collaboratively develop online behavior expectations. The common element is starting with an open and honest conversation about what we want these spaces to be like. Most of the students we have worked with have been remarkably aware of what constitutes appropriate vs inappropriate behavior in online spaces - even as young as Kindergarten.

There are many ways to start this kind of conversation, but one of the easiest is to provide a visible prompt for students to discuss. You can find three of our favorite YouTube videos, that we've been using for years, on this playlist. If you're interested in seeing how we use these videos, check out this series of blog posts) from Kim's time at the International School Bangkok:

- Learning to Blog the Elementary Way
- Blogging Is Elementary
- Student Blogging Guidelines

If none of these videos strike your fancy, there are articles, videos and media segments quite literally multiple times a day about young people (and often adults) behaving badly on social media. You can use anything that you think will resonate with your students to start this kind of conversation. Whatever prompt you use, you'll want to facilitate a conversation that helps students recognize the importance of:

- Thinking before you post
- Considering who will see what they post, and what those people may think
- Some information should always remain private
- Public information should be appropriate to say within a classroom environment (when the teacher is listening)

Being Prepared To Learn

Along these lines, it's worth clarifying (and coming to a common understanding as a class) about what it looks like when you're prepared to learn. If your students take their devices home (in a 1:1 setting for example) some realistic expectations could be:

- Bringing your device charged every day
- Bringing your charger if you know the battery doesn't last all day
- Taking care of your device (carry it safely, run regular software updates, store it in a secure location when you're not using it)

As you get deeper into your connected classroom experience, you'll notice that there are regular opportunities to unpack appropriate, safe and responsible behavior online, and that there are many parallels to face-to-face behavior. We recommend taking advantage of these opportunities as often as you can - and there's no need to wait until you have the devices out in front of you.

You can talk about good behavior anytime. The more you can make the connections between digital and physical in this context, the better!

This is the QR Code to access any content that is in blue type & underlined.

It will direct you to a page on our edurolearning.com website that is password-protected.

To access the content, use the password: **Edur0ycc**

4 MANAGING YOUR CONNECTED CLASSROOM

Classroom management is a challenging skill at the best of times! Thankfully managing a classroom with technology is almost the same as managing a non-technology classroom with some ever-so-slight modifications.

There are a few specific practices that can help you be effective and efficient at managing all the devices in your classroom - and helping your students do the same. The foundation of all of these practices are to think about the expectation you can set to help students use their technology for learning, rather than trying make a rule for every challenge that may arise with the use of devices.

Here are some of our favorites:

Identify Shared Devices By Numbers
If you are using laptop or tablet carts, and students don't have their own devices, it makes sense to try to ensure that they get the same laptop or tablet every time they use them. Even if everything is stored in the cloud (via Google Apps or Office 365) you can cut down on laptop collection and storage time by routinely ensuring that they're using the same device every time. If you have iPads or tablets with locally stored data (like video or audio) this is critical. You can easily stick a number on each device, and then assign each student a number, this way they use the same device each lesson.

Lower Your Lids
Our favorite strategy is to ensure that when you need students attention, you get it. You can do this by asking students to lower (or fully close) their lids whenever you need their attention. Lowering or closing the

lid depends on the device, if they start up quickly (like a Mac), we recommend you have them close their lids all the way. If there are problems starting the device back up again if you close the lid, you might have them lower them to 45 degrees instead. If you have iPads or tablets, you might say "Apples Up". Once you start doing this, it will become habit and you won't even need to ask after a few lessons.

Green / Red Cards on the Door / Bulletin Board
As simple as a stop light. The red / green cards communicate to students - without you having to say a thing - if it's OK to be using their device at the start of your lesson. If your lesson is going to be technology heavy, and you want students logged in and ready to go at the beginning of the lesson, post the green card. If you need student attention at the beginning of the lesson and you want to make sure lids are down, post the red card.

Remove Earphones
Generally speaking, we don't mind if students listen to music while they work - especially if it helps them focus. We've all had individual students who work much better when listening to white noise - so sometimes it's not even music! But, having earphones in sometimes means that students can't even hear you ask for their attention. So, you can use a similar system to the red and green cards (see above), or you can chunk your class time (see below) so that there are specific sections when they're working independently versus listening and interacting with you.

Chunk Class Time
We almost always recommend that students are engaged in individualized learning experiences that are purposeful and student centered. This means that each student may be doing something different during your lesson, and this can be a noisy, busy, environment.

To keep things running smoothly, you might want to chunk your class time so that students know when they're going to get directions, when they can work collaboratively and when they should be working independently.

You can post the agenda on the board, so they know in advance, or you can simply make a habit of how you structure your class time. Most importantly, it does take awhile to settle in to any work using a device, so it's good to ensure that you have enough time to actually make progress on a task during any given lesson.

Purposeful Use of Technology
We always recommend that your use of technology has a clear and transparent purpose, that you're not using technology for technology's sake when you could more effectively use pencil and paper, for example.

Having a purpose to your use helps students stay on task when they have independent or collaborative work time. You may want to help students identify that purpose so that it is explicit and clear to everyone in the room. You can read more about purposeful use in Chapter 5.

Engaging Learning
Along with purposeful use, technology will always be a distraction if the task at hand is not engaging to your learners. Designing learning experiences which require students to use technology to achieve a goal or task that could not be done without technology is a great way to ensure that the learning is engaging. Providing student choice, ownership and differentiation are all successful strategies for engaging your learners as well. You can read more about this in Chapter 5.

Move Around The Room
Our number one tip to manage distractions (with or without technology) is to move around the room. Rather than sitting at a desk or a table group for an extended period of time, make sure that you can regularly see what's going on on your student's screens. If students are off task, you'll start to notice their quick keyboard shortcuts as you get close. This is a great conversation starter to have them show you their browser tabs or windows, or their desktop spaces so you can see what they've been working on. Even if you have the capability to see every student's' screen from your desk, you can not go wrong with walking around the room and interacting with your students as they work.

Ask 3 Before Me
Instead of being the only source of tech help in the room, you can teach your students to ask 3 other students before coming to you. We'll also often suggest ask 3+G (3 people plus Google) before asking the teacher. It's very likely that their peers (or a Google search) will know the answer so there's no need to interrupt you with each technical question.

Utilize Techxperts
We highly recommend the use of "techxperts" in your class. These can be students who are either naturals with technology or a small group of students specifically trained by the teacher to be able to help others with programs, apps or skills. This helps eliminate the stress of being "the expert" and having to help every single student who may get stuck while using technology. Once you've identified your techxperts, and they can change with the tools you're using, you can put up posters so everyone in the room knows who to go to for support.

Tech Breaks / Timers
There is considerable research around the concept of a tech break. No, it's not what you think. The idea is to provide students with time to actually check their tech - so that they can focus when it's time to work.

This works especially well with homework, so it's a great strategy to provide to parents, but it also can work with independent work time in the classroom. You can give students a five minute break to check their social media for every 25 minutes of focused work. If you want to try this strategy, it's great to put a timer on the board so students can see how long they have (both for the working time and the break). Simply google "25 minute timer" and Google's integrated countdown timer will pop up.

Self-Monitoring Apps
There are tons of apps to help students self monitor and restrict their browsing access based on their individual needs. There are timers to help them with tech breaks (like Tomato Timer using the Pomodoro technique), and there are apps that block certain websites for specific durations of time (like Self Control). Self Control has been a favorite with our students for the last 8 years - it works so well that sometimes students block a website (like YouTube) for the whole school day and then can't complete a class activity because they need YouTube - it's that good! These apps are constantly in development and changing all the time, so if you're looking for something specific, we recommend a quick google search!

Know Your Tech Support
If you are in the fortunate situation of having a tech support team physically located in your building, it's well worth knowing who they are, what they offer, and how they work. Some schools will encourage sending students down for support, while others prefer a ticket system. Your tech support team can be a huge lifesaver, so treat them well and follow the rules, they will appreciate your efforts too!

These simple, yet easy to manage, expectations pre-empt many of the issues that can arise when managing a connected classroom. However, every classroom is different so please feel free to add and/or remove any rules that are/aren't needed for you and your students.

Extra Resources:

- Printable Infographic
- Classroom Posters (all of these strategies)
- Top 10 Tips for a Successful Connected Classroom (Video)
- Google Slides Template (Make a Copy)
- Helping Parents Understand Your Connected Classroom (Video)

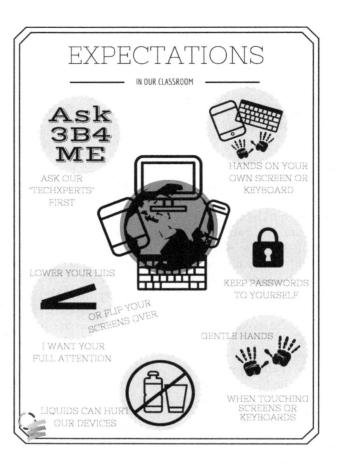

EXPECTATIONS

IN OUR CLASSROOM

Ask 3B4 ME
ASK OUR "TECHXPERTS" FIRST

HANDS ON YOUR OWN SCREEN OR KEYBOARD

LOWER YOUR LIDS
OR FLIP YOUR SCREENS OVER
I WANT YOUR FULL ATTENTION

KEEP PASSWORDS TO YOURSELF

GENTLE HANDS

LIQUIDS CAN HURT OUR DEVICES

WHEN TOUCHING SCREENS OR KEYBOARDS

This is the QR Code to access
any content that is in blue type & underlined.

It will direct you to a page on
our edurolearning.com website
that is password-protected.

To access the content, use the password:

Edur0ycc

5 DESIGNING TECHNOLOGY-RICH LEARNING EXPERIENCES

Although we're already at chapter 5, this is probably the most important part of ensuring your connected classroom is a success! Connecting your classroom is not really about the tech, it's about the learning. And we love talking (and writing) about learning. We love it so much that we created our own unit planner format, called the Authentic Purposeful Learning Experiences (APLE) Unit Planner, that will help you design effective and engaging technology rich learning experiences that will make the most of your connected classroom!

We are especially proud of this unit planner because we have combined four key foundational pedagogical approaches into our APLE unit planner, to create a streamlined and effective way to help you design units that:

- are **authentically** engaging and relevant for your students
- include the **purposeful** use of technology to transform learning
- require your students to **experience** the process of creating something
- lead to student success through a logical structure for product creation

To create this unit planner we have built on four foundational models that we think are essential to a creating an engaging learning environment for students. As you review the unit planner, you'll see strong ties to:

- Understanding by Design
- Project Based Learning (or any of the other similar styles like problem or challenge based learning)
- The SAMR Model
- The MYP Design Cycle

Combining these four foundational models into one unit planning process, with a strong focus on making sure the content is relevant to your students, allows you to design units that will not only engage your students, but also provide structure and support for demonstrating learning through the creation of new and interesting products.

Bonus!
We're so excited about this unit planner that we created a video introduction. If you prefer to watch than read, check it out here!

Key To Success

The key to success with using this unit planner, is to mentally toss out whatever you've done before and start from scratch. Forget about your curriculum documents and resources, start with just the end goal: what you want students to know and be able to do, and develop from there. The idea behind this is to give you the freedom to re-imagine the unit completely differently than you may have taught it before.

In fact, using this process, you might find yourself doing very little direct instruction, and instead providing experiences for students to engage with the content through different media, and then demonstrating their learning through an authentic project.

Get Started

We recommend starting with a unit that hasn't been working well in the past (if you have units where students are loving their learning, demonstrating solid understanding and creating great finished work, why change those?). Pick one that has been challenging - either you don't like how it works, your students consistently struggle with the content, or it's just time to change something up. This will also help you open your mind to new possibilities, and teaching differently than you might have before.

Here's how the four foundational elements of our unit planner all fit together, with some tips for how to use the planner as you design your unit:

Standards
(Understanding by Design)
To make sure that we are keeping our unit focused on the learning targets, the first stage of planning your unit is determining what you would like students to know and be able to do by the end of the unit. To keep a really clear focus on those goals, we start with the relevant standards that will be assessed, just like UbD.

 Tip: In order to truly assess understanding of content, you only want to include the standards here that you will actually assess. Sometimes we get carried away and list all of the standards we might talk about or tangentially cover. These boxes should only include the actual standards that will be assessed. This will help you and your students stay focused.

 **Extra**: You'll notice that we included three types of standards - use the standards that are relevant for you and your students. The ISTE standards are included to help identify opportunities for technology use within your unit. We've selected the ISTE standards for students because they are the most widely respected and utilized in schools around the world.

 Extension: Not only does ISTE have standards for students, but they also have them for teachers and administrators - just in case you're curious about technology expectations for the adults in your building too!

Authentic Learning
Once you've identified your standards, along with what you want students to know and be able to do, you'll see we've provided a section for you to reflect on how to make this particular content relevant to your students. You might want to think about how your specific content connects to the world today, where they might experience your content in their everyday lives, or how they might be affected by the content in the real world.

 **Tip**: This is the key to student engagement. If we, as teachers, can't see how our subject material relates to the real world, it will be very challenging for our students to make the connection. You might want to start by thinking about how you apply your content area in your personal life, or thinking about what will be relevant for students beyond their school career.

Essential Questions & Outcomes (Understanding By Design)
Once you have that authentic connection determined, we head back into a modified Understanding by Design process to identify an **essential question** that can be shared with students, posted in the classroom and in digital spaces, and referred to throughout the unit. This question will be your guide as your students are learning, a reference point that can be discussed regularly.

 Tip: Make sure your essential question is not "Googleable" - you don't want students to be able to search for the answer online, it should be an open question that inspires curiosity and fosters genuine interest. The time you spent thinking about the authentic learning aspect of this unit will help you develop a relevant and relatable question.

After you have your standards put into authentic context and a question that will guide you through your unit, you can think about what you want students to know and be able to do at the end of this unit. What content should they be walking away with? What skills should they have? This will lead you directly into the next section.

Authentic Product (Project Based Learning)
This is when we start thinking about what students will actually create during this unit. You've identified your content standards, as well as the skills and knowledge you want your students to walk away with. Now is the time to determine what they can actually create to demonstrate their understanding.

The goal here is to allow students some creative expression - not necessarily to force everyone in the class to create exactly the same thing (plus we all know how much more interesting it is to provide feedback on unique products, rather than 25 versions of the same thing). The finished product doesn't have to be technology-rich, but this is an opportunity for you to think of new and unique ways for students to demonstrate their learning, which could include the use of technology.

At this point, you want to be thinking about the most interesting and relevant way that students can demonstrate their understand to you, and possibly a wider audience, at the end of the unit. Everything else in this planner will be breaking down the steps it takes to create this product. This means the product should be complicated enough that it will take almost the duration of the unit to create it (when it's broken down into steps), and so that it's interesting enough to explore for the entire time-span of the unit.

Project Ideas:

- Remix video
- Animated gif
- Presentation Zen style presentation
- Blog post
- Infographic
- Public Service Announcement

Tip: Can the product they create also be something that's relevant in their world? Can it be something that students would enjoy creating because they see examples of it in their everyday lives?

Purposeful Use of Technology (SAMR)

You might want to think about the use of technology at the same time as you're thinking about the authentic product, but the finished product does not have to be technology-based. If you're asking students to create something that is technology-rich, you may want to think about how you can move along in the SAMR model.

Tip: As you think about SAMR, don't try to make every single lesson redefinition. It's almost impossible to make a single lesson redefinition, instead, think about your use of technology throughout the project. Your students may experience all levels of SAMR throughout this one unit. It makes the most sense to think about the final product that students will create as the piece that is redefinition, this gives you (and them) lots of time to use technology in new and different ways.

Stages of Learning (MYP Design Cycle)

For the rest of the unit planner, you're going to break down the process of creating that final product into steps. Instead of thinking about front-loading, content delivery, homework, classwork, and then assessment, instead you're going to think about how you would want students to create that final product and break that process down into steps. During each step, you can provide learning experiences for students to dive deeper into your content, as well as provide opportunities for formative assessment.

Each stage should be a building block to completing the final product. Imagine if you were creating this product yourself, almost without the guidance of a teacher, what would you need to do to be successful? Those are the kind of learning experiences we want to facilitate in this process. As a teacher in this classroom, your role will be to break each stage down into smaller steps so students have concrete guidance for how to move through the process, as well as provide essential resources, documentation strategies, feedback and content expertise.

Because you are going to take time now to break down the process of completing each stage, and design learning experiences (that will allow opportunities for feedback), you will find that during the actual teaching of the unit you are facilitating those experiences, rather than directly teaching. Basically this means more work in the planning stages, and less pressure during the actual teaching time.

One of the benefits of teaching this way is that there are many opportunities to pause and reflect throughout the process. We recommend providing specific deadlines at the end of each stage (although you may have shorter term deadlines in the middle of each stage based on the tasks and learning experiences you develop), so that at the end of each stage you provide specific and concrete feedback to each student about their work in relation to what has been completed as well as the work in process toward the finished product. Feedback can be provided in whatever way makes the most sense in your classroom - we've done conferencing, rubrics, video feedback, Google Doc comments, handwritten notes, anything and everything works!

It's worth noting that although we have numbered each stage (for convenience), you can always have students move back and forth between the stages as needed. You can even go back to Stage 1, if the final feedback or reflection prompts more valuable thinking.

 Tip: This may be totally different than how you currently teach, and that's OK. Give it a try and see what you think! We have found that once teachers get the hang of this style, they are really able to take risks and try new things and their students feel very engaged in the process.

 **Extension**: You may want to think about whether you are giving formative feedback at the end of each stage or summative. Based on your subject area, there might be specific standards you need to assess (like research skills, for example) that could be summatively assessed after the first stage, which is fine. Alternatively, you might do all formative assessment until the actual creation of the product, which is when all standards are summatively assessed.

Defining the Stages
As we break down suggested learning experiences for each stage, please note that you can combine and include as many experiences as you feel are necessary, each one having a specific deadline (smaller deadlines within the larger stage), so that students get feedback on each task they complete.

Exploration (Research): Learning Stage 1
This stage introduces the concept to your students, ideally through some kind of hook or interesting starter at the very beginning of the unit. Once they are engaged, this stage provides the framework for student-led investigation into the subject area.

This will most likely be the stage where students learn the most content. The key behind the success of this stage is not deliver content to students, but to provide lots of different media and resources that students can explore and interact with to develop their own understanding.

Ideas for Learning Experiences:

- Determine the problem you're trying to solve
- Research & take notes
- Compile citations
- Explore examples of completed projects
- Determine success criteria

You can choose to have students do all of these things, a few of them, or come up with your own ideas. The goal is to provide students with opportunities to explore and experience the content and to document their developing understanding through the process so that you have a window into what they know about your content by the end of this stage.

Tip: For each of these tasks you might want to create a template for students to complete to document their learning. This provides structure for them as they explore, it also ensures that students are examining all facets of the content that are critical for your subject area. Additionally, it will provide a clear framework for class discussions so that students can all explore different content but come to shared understandings because of the structure they've used.

Tip: If you are asking or allowing students to use a new technology for their final product, you may also want to include some time during this stage to explore with the new tool so they know how to use it and what a reasonable expectation will be for their ability level in the final product.

Finding Pathways (Planning): Learning Stage 2

At this point, students will have developed some strong content understanding and have documented their thinking about the subject area. They will (ideally) be inspired by the product idea that they are expected to create and they will be ready to start planning what their finished product could look like.

The purpose of this stage is to force students to stop and plan out their finished product before they start to actually create. We all know that when we plan something before starting to create it, that the creation process goes much more smoothly.

This stage will not only teach students how to plan successfully, but it will also give you a clear insight into what their finished product will look like before they actually spend the time to make it. This is a great way to scaffold students for success - by giving them feedback on how their concept of their finished product is developing, before so much time has been invested.

Ideas for Learning Experiences

- Student-created timeline of tasks needed to finish the final product
- Storyboard
- Rough Draft
- Outline
- Student-created rubric (or self-assessment) for the final product

 **Tip**: This is usually the stage students have the most trouble with. They want to get started right away and may not see the value of planning. The more you can do to highlight the power of planning "in real life" in your subject area, the more relevant planning will be for your students. For example: whenever we have students create videos, we show them clips of actual Hollywood movie storyboards, here are two of our favorites: Monsters Inc Storyboard Comparison, Lord of the Rings Film to Storyboard Comparison, and two great storyboard resources: Pixar Storyboarding Mini Documentary, Intro to Storyboarding by Rocketjump School

Experiencing (Creating): Learning Stage 3

This is it! This is the stage everyone is always excited about. This is when students actually create the finished product they've been planning for so long. They should be well-planned and organized by now. You as the teacher should have a good idea of how the finished products will turn out. If there were any issues during the Finding Pathways stage, they should be identified so students can address them when they actually create their products.

Usually during this stage, we recommend providing in-class work time for students. This will help you get a good understanding of how they're progressing. It will also teach them how to break down a bigger process into smaller time chunks (since they'll most likely have to do some work at home and some work at school over the course of several days), and it will give you an opportunity to check in with each student over the course of the work periods. Another great thing about in-class work time is, if you've chosen a technology-rich final product, (like the list below), if students have technical trouble, they can get support from other students in class, and you can learn too!

Ideas for Final Products:

- Remix video
- Animated gif
- Presentation Zen style presentation
- Blog post
- Infographic
- Public Service Announcement

Note: you already selected which type of product your students would create during the Authentic Product step above.

 **Tip**: In the past, the creating part may have taken the longest for students, but now with this new structure, you might notice that the first two stages are quite long because that's the most content-dense part of the unit. This stage is all about demonstrating understanding, rather than taking the time to acquire content. Because students should be fairly knowledgeable and organized from the first two stages, this is just a matter of actually doing the work to bring it all together.

Scrapbooking (Reflecting and Evaluating): Learning Stage 4

This is the stage we often skip when following "traditional" unit design, because once we have our assessment completed, we feel the need to move on to the next unit. However, we like to highlight this part of the process because we want students to have the opportunity to receive feedback from a variety of audiences, and ideally, an authentic audience of others who have created similar products.

Ideas for Feedback Opportunities:

- Feedback survey by peers
- Video journal self reflection
- Self-assessment using student created rubric

 Tip: You might want to provide different styles of self reflection for different students. Some feel more comfortable talking about their learning (so a video or audio recording works great), others would rather write, and still others would like to have a conversation with you. If you can differentiate the format of feedback, sometimes the depth of reflection improves right along with it.

Additional Resources

We hope this is a helpful guide to planning authentic, purposeful learning experiences for your students! Just in case you're looking for a little more, here are a few additional resources:

- APLE Guide
- APLE Unit Planner (Master template)
- Designing Learning Experiences
- The Great Design Challenge: Introducing the Design Cycle
- Creating Independent Learners: The Design Cycle
- The Perfect Match: Technology Integration and Understanding by Design

Remember you can access the digital content here.

Use the password:
Edur0ycc

6 QUESTIONS TO ASK YOURSELF
WHEN CREATING A TECH-RICH LESSON

HOW IS WHAT I'M ASKING MY STUDENTS TO DO RELEVANT TO THEIR LIVES TODAY?

What aspects allow students to tie the knowledge and understanding back to their personal lives in the time period for which they live? If a student was to ask you "why does this matter to me today?" what would your answer be?

WHAT KEY KNOWLEDGE AND SKILLS WILL MY STUDENTS ACQUIRE AS A RESULT OF THIS AND HOW WILL I MEASURE THOSE?

The task must be designed and directly linked to having students be able to achieve the understandings, answer the essential questions, and demonstrate the desired outcomes.

WHAT PURPOSEFUL AND AUTHENTIC TASK WILL ALLOW MY STUDENTS TO DEMONSTRATE THEIR UNDERSTANDING(S)?

Task is designed at least at the applying level or higher on Bloom's Taxonomy. Examples are: Creating a new product; Justifying a stand or decision; Distinguishing between different parts; Using information in a new way

HOW DOES THIS TASK REDEFINE OR TRANSFORM STUDENT LEARNING?

Using the SAMR Model of Technology Integration, the technology used allows for significant redesign of a task (Modification) or a new task now possible because of the use of technology (Redefinition)

ARE MY STUDENTS CREATING A PRODUCT / PRODUCING QUALITY WORK USING PROFESSIONAL TOOLS?

Choose the right/best tool for the job! Will the technology tool(s) help students produce quality work and meet the learning objectives?

IS THERE AN OPPORTUNITY TO SHARE AND/OR GET FEEDBACK ON OUR LEARNING GLOBALLY?

Opportunities to share learning helps build authentic audience and purposeful learning. It also raises the quality of work and can be very motivating for students to know others are looking at their work.

COETAIL
A COMMUNITY APPROACH TO LEARNING
www.coetail.com

eduro
www.edurolearning.com

6 MEDIA LITERACY IN YOUR CONNECTED CLASSROOM

One of the fantastic hidden advantages (or maybe not so hidden, depending on your perspective) of creating a connected classroom is the opportunity to teach media and digital literacy in an authentic and purposeful environment.

Our students use the internet everyday in so many different ways, but generally speaking they are usually better at using connected technologies for social interaction, gaming and consumption of media, rather than for academic purposes. When you have access to this kind of technology in your classroom you can take advantage of their enthusiasm, engagement and energy around the use of the internet and all sorts of apps, while making the connection to purposeful use, safe and responsible behavior, and using technology to make the world a better place. Those sound like lofty goals, but we promise, they are possible!

This section will cover a selection of essential skills for success in our digital world. This isn't an exhaustive list, but these are the skills we think are most important when you're starting out.

Skill 1: Reading a Google Search Results Page

Your students use Google everyday. Most likely no one has taught them how to read the results, the way we teach them to read the index section or table of contents of a book. It may seem simple, but it's important to take time to go over the index page with students. Just like the index section of a book, there are different parts to a google search results page. It's good to know what they are, what they do and why they are there.

Here's what you'll find:

Note: Google is constantly changing the way that results are returned. Your results may differ from someone else's.

- Quick Overview at the top (this will usually include a definition of the term you search for, or a series of questions that dig deeper and provide quick response answers)
- Top Stories (providing relevant, up to date stories in the news related your search term)
- Search Results (the list of websites Google has returned based on your keywords)
- Advertising/Ads

Note: Google explanation for the appearance of ads is "If we think an ad will help you find what you're looking for, we might show ads on the top of the results page or on the right side. You'll know it's an ad and not a search result because of the yellow Ad or Ads icon next to the URL."

Key Elements to Understand:

Every search result has three parts:

1. **Title:** Usually blue, and is hyperlinked (what you click on). It's the title of the web page; and is a clue of what we're probably going to find on that web page.

2. **URL:** Web Address (URL) of the web page, in green (can explain to students that just everyone's home has it's own address, so too do pages on the internet (web).

3. **Snippet:** The text that helps show how the page relates to your search query. Roughly 25 words or so showing what's on that web page around your search terms (your search term is generally in bold, its purpose is to help you decide if the page has what you're looking for)

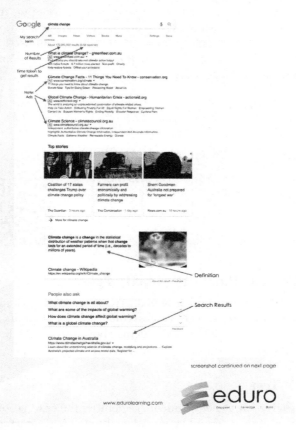

screenshot continued on next page

www.edurolearning.com

Additional Resources

- [Teaching Students How To Read A Search Result Page](#) (Video)
- [Teaching Students How To Read a Search Result Page](#) (PDF)

This is the QR Code to access any content that is in blue type & underlined.

It will direct you to a page on our edurolearning.com website that is password-protected.

To access the content, use the password: **Edur0ycc**

Skill 2: Focus Searching for Students

Sometimes we forget that Google automatically creates a filter bubble of our searches based on the information it already knows about us, thanks to previous searches we've done, websites we've visited and personalizations we've made by being logged into our Google account. We think you can use this type of lesson with Grades 4 and up, but could be adapted for Grade 3 as long as you adjust your search terms and language.

Additional Resources

- Focused Searching for Students (Video)
- Focused Searching for Students (PDF)

You can access the
digital content with this QR code.

Use the password:
Edur0ycc

Skill 3: Does it Pass the CARP Test?

How do you know what's true is actually true? Learning how to critically evaluate information resources is an essential skill for students undertaking academic research. Teaching your students about the CARP Test is a starting point for evaluating information resources.

The CARP Test

CARP is an acronym to help students remember the criteria for evaluating sources. Older students could be introduced to CRAAP (currency, relevance, authority, accuracy and purpose) "hooked" with the added bonus of the play on words.

An Elementary (Primary) teacher has also used PARCA (pronounced par-ka) to associate the protective nature of a parka from the wind and rain (the fake news) for their students.

What is CARP?

Currency - the timeliness of the information

Is the information current enough for your topic? If students are seeking data from World War II, then facts written in 2005 would probably suffice. But if students are doing a project on the planets and find articles from 2005, there could be some misinformation. That's because in 2006, the definition of a planet changed, which meant that Pluto was no longer considered a planet. So, in order to make sure students are accurately finding information, they should think about the topic they are searching and how up-to-date the information needs to be.

Ask yourself:

- When was it published?
- Has it ever been Updated?
- Any newer articles published on this topic
- Is this a topic that changes rapidly (ie: technology, pop culture)

Authority - the source of the information
Who wrote the information? Are they a trustworthy source? Is it some random person you've never heard of or is it someone or an organization or company that is well-respected (or maybe NOT well-respected)? Are credentials provided?

Ask yourself:

- Who is the author/publisher/sponsor of the source?
- What are their "credentials" / "qualifications"
- Is the author qualified to write on this topic?
- Are there any other experts in the field to look up?
- Are other sites linking to this site?

Reliability - the accuracy of the information
Where was the information found? Was it an .edu site? .gov? .com? .net? Teaching students what these extensions mean will help them quickly identify the reliability of a site and where it is coming from. For example, if students see the URL ends in .gov, they will know it's coming from a government and should therefore be pretty reliable. If it ends in .net or .com, it may be a business that is selling something, which could either be reliable or not. It's best to compare the information found on these sites with other sites.

Ask yourself:

- Are there any obvious falsehoods that you can see?
- Has the information ever been reviewed by other experts?
- What citations or references support the information given?
- What do others say about the same topic?
- Are there relevant links to other sites?

Along these lines, it's always good to check your information with multiple sources. It can be so easy to find what you want to be true, also called confirmation bias. By confirming what you read by finding it in more than one place, you are doing your part as a critical consumer of information.

Purpose/Point of View - the reason the information exists

What is the author's purpose in writing the information? To entertain? To inform? To persuade? To sell? It's important to teach students to not just click on the first link in their search query, as it's most likely an ad. Many students do not know the difference.

Ask yourself:

- What is the purpose? Sell? Persuade? Inform? Entertain?
- Are there political, religious, ideological, cultural, institutional and/or personal biases?
- Any alternative points of view shared?
- Strong or emotional language used?

Along with the CARP Test, we encourage you to empower your students to be participatory citizens, creating & publishing truthful information for the public. It's vital to remember that rather than just consumers, we hope our students are creators! We do not have to just sit back and be the victim of fake news. We can teach our students to be proactive and publish high quality, reliable information for the world to benefit.

The amount of information available online is so vast, so it's imperative that students innately analyze their sources before accepting and using the information.

Additional Resources

- Does it Pass the CARP Test? (Poster)
- Critical Thinking Cheatsheet (Printable)
- Checking the Authenticity of a Website (Video)

You can access the digital content using the QR code above.

Use the password:
Edur0ycc

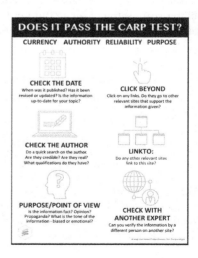

DOES IT PASS THE CARP TEST?

CURRENCY   AUTHORITY   RELIABILITY   PURPOSE

CHECK THE DATE
When was it published? Has it been revised or updated? Is the information up-to-date for your topic?

CLICK BEYOND
Click on any links. Do they go to other relevant sites that support the information given?

CHECK THE AUTHOR
Do a quick search on the author. Are they credible? Are they real? What qualifications do they have?

LINKTO:
Do any other relevant sites link to this site?

PURPOSE/POINT OF VIEW
Is the information fact? Opinion? Propaganda? What is the tone of the information - biased or emotional?

CHECK WITH ANOTHER EXPERT
Can you verify the information by a different person on another site?

An Example:

Using the CARP test to evaluate a Wikipedia article

Currency

- Use the [View history] tab on a Wikipedia article to check when it was created, and whether it has been kept up-to-date
- Review the publication dates on the references at the end of the article

Authority

- All statements in Wikipedia should be facts backed up by references to reputable third-party sources.
- A quality article should have no [citation needed] flags, and a quality reference list.
- Readers can check who has made edits on an article in the [View history] tab by clicking on the editor's username and a link to the editor's other Wikipedia contributions

Reliability

- While vandalism and spam can be an issue for Wikipedia, every edit is recorded, and all versions can be easily restored
- There are automated filters plus human patrollers who monitor recent edits and pages of interest to them
- Wikipedia has a checklist of <u>reliability criteria</u> that considers accuracy of information, appropriateness of images, style and focus of articles, exclusion and removal of false information, comprehensiveness, scope and coverage, susceptibility to editorial and systemic bias, and quality of writing

Purpose/Point of view

- Wikipedia is an encyclopedia, written from a neutral point of view
- Its content should include facts, not opinions.
- To check for debates and contentious issues related to topics, click on the [Talk page] of an article and read the discussion.

Wikipedia is just one source educators can use to help students build their referencing and critical thinking skills.

Adapted from teachermagazine.com.au

www.edurolearning.com

Skill 4: Embracing Digital Citizenship

Digital Citizenship is pretty much exactly what it sounds like: behaving as a good citizen in digital spaces. Basically we mean safe, responsible and respectful behavior online. As teachers, we are great about teaching these skills in our traditional face-to-face classroom environment. Now it's time to take those skills and draw connections and parallels to behaviors in the digital world.

It can seem intimidating to talk about behavior in online spaces, especially when our students are often using apps that we know nothing about, but actually, you already have all the skills you need with the added bonus of life experience and a fully developed pre-frontal cortex to put things into context and make sound judgements.

Some key elements worth exploring with your students are:

Private vs Public Sharing

We love the idea of students demonstrating and sharing their learning in public spaces, but every time we ask students to share, we need to make sure we're also asking them to think before they post. What elements of their work (or their personal lives) are safe to share to a public audience? What should be kept private? How do we make that choice? A great rule of thumb to share with students is that anything shared online should be something that your students should feel comfortable saying in the classroom, with the teacher listening. We also like the guideline of making sure your grandmother and your teacher would approve.

Digital Footprint

When thinking about what is shared in public spaces, it's worth mentioning (or facilitating a conversation which helps students come to the understanding that) everything we post becomes part of our "digital footprint". We want to leave behind steps that show us in the most positive light, which means we need to make the choice about what we share before we publish.

Creating Classroom Guidelines for Behavior

See the "Setting Expectations for Behavior" section in Chapter 3: Creating Your Connected Classroom for background. You can build upon this discussion by taking the conversation further, to public digital spaces. In essence the expectations should be exactly the same, but you might want to think and talk about the extra level of clarity and communication required when we're collaborating and sharing with people we might not know in a face-to-face setting.

Respectfully Disagreeing as Resilient Digital Citizens

Learning how to be respectful and resilient in the digital age is tough. Research out of Harvard's Berkman Klein Center tells us that in order to combat the cruelty of the offline & online worlds, we need to "empower youth to create a kinder and braver world." One of the strategies they suggest to eradicate bullying is to develop students' interpersonal skills.

In our Respectfully Disagreeing as Resilient Digital Citizens online course video we chat with ES Counselor at the International School of Kuala Lumpur, Chris Wright, shares her top tips for building resiliency in students:

Let kids try things and let them fail
Mistakes are a huge part of learning! It's ok to try something and not succeed - but it's not ok to not try.

Be reflective
Give multiple opportunities for students to reflect on those mistakes and apply as new learning.

Model and expect active listening
It's okay to disagree, but it's important to respectfully acknowledge what someone else is saying.

Teach mindfulness
Be focused in the moment and on the conversation. Before having a reactive response, teach kids to give themselves time to think and respond appropriately.

At the heart of what empathy is, seeking to understand before being understood is the key to building relationships and tolerance, opening the door to more respectful communication.

One of the biggest challenges a digital citizenship curriculum can address is the way we interact with each other - both online and offline. We know that it's much easier to react anonymously and not have to be held accountable for our actions. But is that the right thing to do? How do we teach our students to have the same integrity in digital spaces as in the physical world?

Cyberbullying

One of the biggest challenges with a technology-rich classroom, and the use of technology tools in general, is the potential for negative interactions with peers. We know that behavior that pushes boundaries is a normal part of growing up, and we know how to handle it in a face-to-face setting. However, although bullying (or just "drama" as teens refer to negative behavior in online spaces) in digital spaces bears many similarities to what we may have experienced growing up in the traditional sense, it has a number of very specific differences that are worth talking about with your students:

- Digital media doesn't "disappear", which means hurtful words or media can be re-read and re-watched (and therefore re-experienced) over and over again. This does not allow the memory to fade with time and can have a bigger impact than face-to-face interactions.

- Digital confrontation can take place anytime. This means negative interactions may not be limited to school hours - or even specific locations. When we take our devices home, or we interact with others via our personal phones, negative behavior can follow us everywhere we go. This often makes it feel like there is no "safe place" where students can just be - their peers can follow them home 24/7.

- Digital confrontation can be hard to "see" and therefore adults don't always know when to intervene. Because it's all taking place on the screen and the adults around them (including their parents) can't see or hear what's happening, they may not be aware that teens need help.

If you are looking for more details on this topic, we highly recommend Danah Boyd's book "It's Complicated" available here as a free PDF

Safety in Online Spaces

Depending on the kind of space you choose to use with your students, it may be possible for others outside of an educational setting to both see what your students are doing, and to interact with them. Although at first this may sound scary, it's a great learning opportunity. Now is the time to talk about making good choices about what we share online (see Public vs Private Sharing above), and to learn resilience and persistence in digital spaces.

It's critical for students to evaluate who they should talk to and what they can share with those individuals. As you facilitate conversations about this, it is worth making the parallel to "stranger danger" in the physical world. You might want to ask questions like:

- Who are you talking to?

- What do you know about them?

- How can you find out more?

- How are they supporting your learning?

You might also want to talk about how we chose to interact with others. If your students are going to be commenting on other students (or experts) work, the way that they exchange those comments should be an important discussion. Please see Chapter 7 for The Comment Sandwich activity you can do with all age levels.

Explicit Media in Online Spaces

Another challenging aspect of using the internet is the ready availability of explicit materials. And sometimes in the most unlikely of places. For example: we've had students research Brazil and come up with lots of images that had nothing to do with what we expected. Instead of letting this become an obstacle to using the internet, this can be a learning experience.

The reality is that students are using the internet all the time, and most likely no one is teaching them how to handle unexpected content (and quite honestly, they may be using search queries that will provide content that they may not be ready for - even if they enter the terms themselves in the keyword search). Even if your internet access at school is heavily filtered, it's unlikely that every single place they access the internet is filtered (think of their 4G access on their phone, or the internet at a friends house, or the internet at Starbucks, or other public wifi). It's critical that students learn to use "the filter between their ears" - even if it's not explicitly necessary in your classroom.

Now is the time to talk to them about their reactions when they see something they think (or know) is not appropriate for them. Our recommended strategy is to close the lid immediately (or turn over the device) and call an adult. This way the adult can still see what was on the screen, so they can make a judgement call about how to handle the situation, but the student is not looking at it any more. It's important for students to know that they won't be punished for what they find, even if it is explicit, because it most likely was not their intention. It's also important to remember that often times, even if they know it's not appropriate for them, they don't have the full context of what they saw, so the simplest explanation is often best.

You can guide your reaction and feedback by asking a few important questions:

- What upset you about this image / video / content?
- What do you think it means?
- What questions do you have?

This is not an easy topic to talk about, but all young people have questions, and some of them may chose your class time to try to find answers. Knowing that this could happen, and how you might handle it will go a long way towards feeling confident in the moment. It's happened to all of us, so we know you can do it!

Citing Sources

Once students have access to the world wide web of information, it becomes even more critical to properly cite and acknowledge source material. While we understand that different schools may have different expectations for citation format (MLA vs ALA for example), at the very least, all teacher should expect a complete URL for any content that they use or reference in their work. Most importantly, google.com (or any URL beginning with google...) is not a source. When we're talking about a complete URL, we mean the actual page where you, as the teacher, can see the information or content your students used. Sometimes this is confusing because we don't always know how to read search results and/or find the actual URL. Please explore the tips earlier in this chapter for more details.

Creative Commons

An amazing resource for teachers and students is Creative Commons. Creative Commons is a licence, like copyright, but different in that it was designed for people who want their work to be used. In essence, Creative Commons is a license that allows anyone to use their creative work. This is amazing for teachers and students because:

1. the content is not a restricted copyright, which means it can be legally used and shared in public spaces. In fact there are several types of licenses included in Creative Commons. To see what they are and how they can be used, visit this link.

2. Anyone can license their work with a Creative Commons license. This means that your students can share and gain recognition for their work. This is a great example to share with your students (as appropriate).

In all honesty, this really is just scratching the surface of digital citizenship, there is so much more to discuss, we could write another book on the topic (and maybe we will!). Hopefully this has highlighted some of the key elements that are worth talking about with your students as you begin your journey.

This is the QR Code to access any content that is in blue type & underlined.

It will direct you to a page on our edurolearning.com website that is password-protected.

To access the content, use the password: **Edur0ycc**

---

7 TAKING YOUR CONNECTED CLASSROOM GLOBAL

Once you have built a PLN and created your connected classroom, you, and your students are ready to connect with a global audience!

As Fernando M. Reimers writes in Leading for Global Competency:

> *Good educators know that the real world is ever more interconnected and interdependent. We all share in facing such planetary challenges as climate change, health epidemics, global poverty, global economic recessions and trade imbalances, assaults on human rights, terrorism, political instability, and international conflicts. We also share opportunities for global collaboration in such areas as scientific and artistic creation, trade, and international cooperation. These challenges and opportunities define the contours of our lives, even in their most local dimensions. Yet in spite of growing awareness of the importance of developing global skills, few students around the world have the opportunity today to become globally competent.*

As exciting and enriching as globally collaborative projects are, it can be a daunting task to start one on your own. The good thing is, you've already started to develop the skills you need by building your Personal Learning Network (Chapter 2) and Connecting Your Class (Chapter 3), so you're ready to take the next step!

We recommend working in phases so that you can build your confidence, and work out any specific kinks or challenges in your school setting as you open your classroom up to the world.

Phase 1: Window Shopping

Before you jump in, it's always worth exploring the types of projects that already exist, to give yourself an idea of what teachers and their students are doing in this space. Here are some projects that we've learned about through our individual PLNs that you can explore.

- Stories of a Lifetime (Jason Mn and Marc Faulder)
- Traveling Ted (Pana Asavavatana)
- Quadblogging (and a great reflection here from Nicki Hambleton)
- A biiiiig list (from Lisa Parisi)
- Writing Matrix (Vance Stephens)
- Podcasts: This I believe (Ceci Gomez-Galvez & Nathan Lill, Shekou International School, China)
- Blog: TIME: Student Led Museum Reflections (Ceci Gomez-Galvez & Nathan Lill, Shekou International School, China)
- Student Creative (David Gran, Shanghai American School, China)
- Our Global Friendships (Lisa Parisi, Toni Olivieri-Barton)

If you like the sound of one of these, you can always request to join in! Or, if none of these seem right to you, you can try a google search to see if there's something more relevant, or you can try to model something simple, similar to one of these, with a teacher you already know (see more about how to get started on a custom collaboration in Phase 4, below).

As you continue to develop your PLN, you'll hear about projects that are relevant to your classroom needs, because the people in your PLN are selected by you!

Phase 2: Getting Comfortable with Global Collaboration

Here are a few types of projects that we think are a great way to start exploring the idea of connecting your class on a global scale.

Option 1: Close Collaboration

To build your confidence and comfort with global projects, you might want to start with a collaboration within your school – either right in your building, or within your district. You could start by simply connecting with another teacher of the same subject and/or grade level and have share and comment each other's work.

The idea with this one, though, is to challenge yourself to do it in a digital space (not face to face, even if the classroom is right next door). It doesn't matter if you start with a collection of Google Docs, or a Twitter hashtag, or commenting on each other's blogs, see if you can build some strategies within a very safe and comfortable environment that will help you eventually branch out to a connection further afield.

Option 2: Virtual Field Trips

A super easy way to break down classroom walls is to take your class on a virtual field trip. Along with saving time not having to plan so many details of a field trip, a virtual field trip gets rid of the geography barriers that traditional field trips bring. Your students can take a virtual tour of the Louvre in France, tour the US National Monuments in Washington, DC, or experience an African safari.

Skype in the classroom offers virtual field trips, which open the potential to visit a place outside of your state or country. The Microsoft Educator Community offers access to a variety of different virtual field trip options This also offers the ability for students to travel around the world without a passport, exposing them to different cultures and languages.

Google Connected Classrooms, a Google+ community, offers a variety of resources for teachers wishing to plan virtual field trips for their students. You can post questions if there is a specific field trip wish you have in mind, or browse for virtual field trips currently being offered. Do you have Google Cardboard? If so, try Google Expeditions, an app for both Android and iOS that utilizes Google Cardboard, and lets you take your students on immersive, virtual journeys.

Many museums also offer a virtual field trip for students to experience a place they might not otherwise get to visit. This website lists a variety of different museums that offer virtual field trips for your students to discover.

You can even virtually travel to another part of the world (depending on what you're studying) using Google Maps. Have a conversation about how this land is different and similar to their own. For example, if students in California are studying drought, travel to a country with a desert in Africa or the Middle East.

Option 3: Video Chat

Another way that you can create global collaboration with your students is to use video chat to connect with others around the world. Connecting with another person or classroom through video brings a fun update to the pen pal. It can also connect your students with people in another country or experts in fields they're studying.

A fun way to connect with another classroom is to participate in a Mystery Skype session. These mystery sessions can take place on Skype or Google Hangouts and are a fun way to connect to other classrooms around the globe. Using yes or no questions, your classroom tries to discover where the classroom you've connected with is in the world. To begin, have your students research about the area you live in – think geography, population, climate. Once you've got this information, your students are ready to solve a mystery! The classroom you've connected with has done similar background research, so classrooms will go back and forth asking yes or no questions until they figure out the location of the other end of the video chat.

Video can help your students through collaborative learning. Although the curriculum varies from school to school, and country to country, talking about general issues that are relevant to your classroom can open your students' eyes to how another country thinks about that topic. Try connecting with a classroom in Europe when learning about European history, or a classroom in Mexico when fine tuning Spanish language skills.

Video chat can also be used to invite a guest to speak with your students. Just like a field trip, sometimes geography hinders us from being able to get a special guest speaker to speak with students. Offering the guest speaker a video chat option can help take the stress off of them, since they can speak with your students from the comfort of their own office or home. The Global Read Aloud is a quick and easy way to get started with a guest speaker (well, reader) in your classroom! Does your class have a book they've enjoyed? Check the author list at Skype an Author Network to see if the book's author will video chat with your classroom!

Here are a few more ideas to try:

- Celebrations
  - » Science Week
  - » Coding Challenge
  - » Holiday tradition comparisons
- Expert Encounters
  - » Guest expert
  - » Author Study
  - » Mystery Skype for geography/cultural purposes

- Shared Units of Study
  - » Weather study/comparison
  - » Seasons
  - » Environmental studies
- Authentic Collaboration Projects
  - » Writing projects
  - » Mascot travels (read one of Sam the Kiwi's weekend adventure with a student)
  - » Music

Sometimes time zones can hamper global connections. Tools like VoiceThread can help.

A great reminder for students is to be patient with the learning process through video chat. Some connections may be poor, especially if you or the other classroom or person you are trying to reach has a poor internet connection, or is relying on a public internet connection. This is just the reality of working with new technologies, and it's always a great opportunity for us to role model patience, resilience, and not getting frazzled when things don't go according to plan!

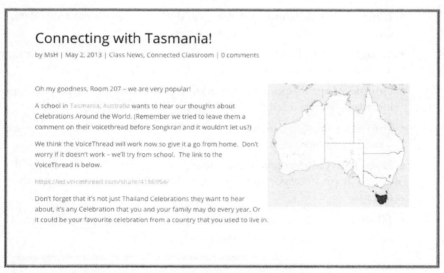

Connecting with Tasmania!

by MsH | May 2, 2013 | Class News, Connected Classroom | 0 comments

Oh my goodness, Room 207 – we are very popular!

A school in Tasmania, Australia wants to hear our thoughts about Celebrations Around the World. (Remember we tried to leave them a comment on their voicethread before Songkran and it wouldn't let us?)

We think the VoiceThread will work now so give it a go from home. Don't worry if it doesn't work – we'll try from school. The link to the VoiceThread is below.

https://ed.voicethread.com/share/4186954/

Don't forget that it's not just Thailand Celebrations they want to hear about, it's any Celebration that you and your family may do every year. Or it could be your favourite celebration from a country that you used to live in.

Chrissy's 3rd Grade class was able to connect and share some Christmas Traditions with a class in Tasmania using VoiceThread to combat time zone issues

Possible student roles during video conferencing:

- **Calendar:** Responsible for adding Date & Time of planned Skype connection to shared & embedded Google Calendar
- **Greeter:** Greets the partner school. Makes initial introduction. Talks about Geographic location.
- **Share:** Shares something special about class, school, city, state or country. Could be song, dance, souvenir, project, sports team, etc.
- **Q & A:** Asks specific questions for data collection. Responsible for keeping conversation fluid
- **Photographer:** Responsible for documenting connection with still images.
- **Videographer:** Responsible for documenting connection with video.
- **Backchannel Writers:** Documenting conversation, questions, answers and classroom happenings during the connection on a backchannel chat (Ex. Today's Meet)
- **Backchannel Cleanup:** Responsible to save backchannel chat as a Word Document and cleaning up duplicate comments and mark questionable statements to be verified.
- **Live Blogger:** Blogs skype call live to classroom blog
- **Blogger Word Problem:** Creates a Math word problem from data, questions and answers collected during skype call
- **Google Earth:** Finds location of skype partner and measures distance in miles & kilometres.
- **Google Map:** Responsible for adding place mark of Skype partner's location to embedded Google Map on classroom blog.
- **Info Station:** Responsible to search for any data question on the spot. Verifies any questionable information as well.
- **Data Entry:** Responsible for adding data collected into embedded google form on classroom blog. Ex. distance miles/km, temperature in F/C.
- **Elapsed time:** Responsible for noting time Skype call started and ended as well as calculating elapsed time

Check out this helpful Infographic from Sylvia Tolisano (Langwitches)

Skype Assigned Roles

Skype/Video Conferencing Tips

These are some tips and tricks we've picked up along the way from our journey of discovery with Skype and Video Conferencing.

Before the skyping/conferencing

- Practise speaking slowly and clearly (it's amazing how many students don't pronounce their words very well)
- If your topic is prearranged – have a list of the students names on the board
- Organise your class to sit in rows with an aisle (makes movement up the camera and mic manageable)
- Place a "speaker chair" in front of the webcam/camera

During the skyping/conferencing

- Don't have your speakers too loud – this is a major cause of feedback
- Encourage your students to say who they are before they continue to speak
- One class asks a question, the other class answers then asks their question etc – an organisational system that seems to work really well
- Use a wikispace / pbwiki / blog to record the results and information from your conversations!

Other Helpful Tips for Skype/Video Conferencing

- We've found that a hand-held mic works very well to help establish one person speaking at a time (you can't speak without the "talking stick")
- Prearrange a student to say thank you for talking with us today
- If possible, test your equipment (without the students)

Phase 3: Open Your Classroom To the World

As you become more and more comfortable with a global classroom, you can share more of the learning that's happening in a variety of spaces. This will allow you to create an environment that is open to the outside world and engages students in real-life authentic learning that can extend to reach other global learners.

Option 1: Blogging

Blogs can be a "window into your class" – an authentic, relevant way to connect to others beyond the four walls of the classroom.

Blogs can be used to

- Share learning
- Have an authentic audience
- Get peer feedback
- build ePortfolios
- Communicate with parents

Ideas to try

- Start with a class blog and build content together
- Use blogs as ePortfolios to show learning over time
- Connect between school and home

Start Small. Begin with a class blog. If an individual blog for each student is too big of a jump for you, you can start with a class blog that you manage, but students have direct responsibilities, like:

- Student Writer of the Week (responsible for writing a summary post or a daily post for the class)
- Blog Photographer (responsible for documenting learning each day)
- Commenting on a class blog post could be a writing homework option
- Blogger of the Week – use when each student has their own blog

Connecting Students Through Blogging - 10 Tips

Get blogging started in your classroom and keep it sustainable throughout the year. Most apply to individual blogs with your students and/or blogging together with students on a class blog.

#1 Decide on your why (the purpose)
It's important to know why you want a class blog or why you want students to have their own blogs. When we know the why (to anything), it's so much easier to make decisions about what and what not to do, and it will be much easier to get students excited about blogging with the goal of sustainability. Don't move onto the how, until you know the why! (It comes in handy for #3)

#2 Pick your platform
This one might end up being entirely up to you or you may not have much of a choice. We've been fortunate enough to work at schools that hosted WordPress on their own servers. When Chrissy first started out with a class blog, she used EduBlogs (free version), and then WordPress (free version) when her students began blogging individually. There are other alternatives out there such as Kidblog or Weebly which many teachers use with great success.

#3 Obtain permissions
In order to receive support from all stakeholders, you need to check in with those around you. Principals, Tech Coach/Co-ordinators, and of course your parents. It's important to be ready to explain what you are doing and why (refer #1). We share a blogging/podcasting contract with parents and also held a parents meeting so that any questions/concerns could be asked and answered. To date, we've not had any parents say no to their child blogging and we're sure it's because of #1, knowing the why and because of the transparency of what we were trying to achieve with blogging.

#4 Teach Quality Blogging
This will always be one of our many favourite sessions with student bloggers and they go hand-in-hand with our Digital Literacy Unit for the start of the year. Our Guiding Question: What makes a quality post? springboards us into blogging and helps students think about the similarities and differences between blogging and writing. We revisit this topic many times during the year and aim to deepen the quality of blog posts through a "writing reflectively" lens.

#5 Discuss Citizenship
Before we even begin blogging, we look at and discuss safety online and citizenship – what does it mean to be responsible and appropriate? This is part of a bigger discussion that covers not only online behaviour but offline behaviour. It just so happens that it's not just those that are specific to blogging – and it's like quality blogging & commenting – an all-the-time discussion. Blogging

#6 Teach commenting
Teaching your students to properly comment is just as important, if not more important as teaching your students about writing quality blog posts. As <u>Pernille Ripp</u>, from <u>Blogging Through the Fourth Dimension</u>, mentions

> *"In order for blogging to be effective, comments are needed, but if students don't know how to properly comment they will lose out on part of the experience. We discuss how to thank people, how to answer their questions, and most importantly, how to ask questions back. This is all part of common conversational knowledge that all kids should be taught any way."*

#7 Start small
Everybody starts somewhere right? Whether you start out with a class blog first, or dive head first into students having their own blog. Be realistic about how much you want to be posting. We always started with an introduction post of some sort like this one or this one (which was fun and really encouraged comments). At first, we posted to our blogs once a week. It was regular and it was consistent – both of these things are important when you're building an audience. (See #8)

#8 Connect with others
There is no doubt that the global connections made with students from all over the world are what inspired and encouraged my students to keep blogging. Reach out to a colleague at another school and ask if their students can read and comment on your blogs – maybe they are blogging too and you can help motivate them too! Have a go at QuadBlogging or use twitter to help you and your students connect to others. Keep a flag counter in your sidebar to help keep visitors to your blog (and your students' blogs) visible and motivating!

#9 Allow personalisation (making it their own)

All students love to explore their blogs, playing with themes, colour and font! This makes for a really great lesson on Design when they teach each other how to do anything fancy and also let each other know when font or colour choices were poor. It's a perfect opportunity for students to start thinking about creating their online identity too. (Don't forget to teach your students about Creative Commons and giving attribution for images they use in their blog posts! – see #5)

#10 Give it time

Rome wasn't built in a day – neither will your blog content or your blog audience! It's an on-going process that can at times seem more trouble than it's worth, but at the same time be so beneficial for students – especially those students who's voices can be hard to hear above others. Stick with it, even when the going gets tough and time pressures seem overwhelming against you. It's worth the effort, honest!

Helpful resources

Mr Mike Jessee and his students at ISBangkok – A great example of a classroom blog in action

Jeff Utecht: Sustained blogging in the Classroom (a 2010 K12Online Conference presentation) with some still very relevant points to consider when blogging in the classroom

Five Steps to Starting a Class Blog – Kathleen Morris

Create A Class Blog – The Edublogger

14 Steps to Meaningful Student Blogging – Pernille Ripp

This is the QR Code to access any content that is in blue type & underlined.

It will direct you to a page on our edurolearning.com website that is password-protected.

To access the content, use the password: **Edur0ycc**

Connecting with Comments

Once you start blogging with your class, you'll want to have your students leave comments for each other, and for other collaborative classrooms. It's important to make sure we take time to teach how to leave a successful comment. This will help students to understand and value the purpose of commenting, and ensure that comments are a meaningful use of class (and homework) time. Check out the Comment Sandwich Lesson Plan to help you get started!

This lesson plan is aimed at Grades 3-5 (also adaptable for older students), working in Google Docs (or something similar like OneNote). Included in this PDF is an optional Comment Sandwich Printable for your students to use.

A compliment/comment sandwich isn't new. In fact, it's a strategy for writing emails as well. We can also call it a digital literacy strategy that can be used whether you are leaving comments on writing, on others' blogs or any digital writing where someone can't see you physically. It's a great strategy to start teaching students.

Option 2: Social Media (with tools like Twitter, Instagram, and Snapchat)

Social media tools can be used to:

- share learning
- participate in global conversations
- ask questions / get answers
- connect with experts, authors, other cultures
- back channel
- expose students to different perspectives

Ideas to try:

- share learning visually with a class instagram account
- create a class twitter account to globally connect with others
- start a class facebook page to connect/share with parents

Tips for Success:

- It takes time to grow connections but it really is worth the effort
- Be willing to take risks (be prepared to fail)
- Be adaptable and flexible and have a sense of humour!
- If you're just starting out, start small – Skype in an expert/guest speaker or your friend's class from another school in your area, district, or perhaps another country.

Start Small: Use a Class Social Media Account. Just like with a class blog, you can dip your toes into the social media waters by creating a class account that you oversee, but students manage.

- The whole class helps write a summary of the day's learning in 140 characters for twitter OR
- A small group of writers during writing time collaborate for 10-15m on a class daily tweet
- Social Media update – to help provide a window into the classroom, a student writes a morning and an afternoon twitter, instagram, facebook update each day
- Instagram Photographer of the day – has to post 4-5 images of learning to the class instagram account
- Facebook Post writer – writes a learning post/summary of the day's learning am/pm (also uses the class photographer's images)

Depending on how old your students are, you may wish to have the posts/updates have teacher approval before they are published. With younger students, updates could be orally told to an adult or written out on paper and approved by the teacher first.

Phase 4: Create a Custom Collaboration

There are tons of ways to collaborate with other classrooms, but the ones we have found to be the most meaningful are the projects we've developed ourselves, in collaboration with another teacher (or more!). Building your PLN is an essential step to success with this one because you need a close connection with at least one other teacher to create a truly custom collaborative project that meets the curricular needs of all classrooms involved.

Here's how to make it happen!

Define Project Goals:

The first step to any successful collaboration is communication. Spend some time – over several days or weeks – discussing what you hope to accomplish and how you might go about completing the project. Make sure that all teachers have time to touch-base with their support personnel in school to ensure that they have the required materials or support. Think about:

- What standards do you need to meet with this project?
- What would you like students to understand?
- What are your essential questions?
- What kind of authentic task can you design for your students to demonstrate their understanding?
- What supporting activities or tasks need to be completed to help your students construct their understanding?

Develop Explicit Expectations:

From the outset clarify what the expectations are for all teachers and students involved in the project. Think about:

- Time commitments
  - » Will this take one lesson or 12?
  - » Is one lesson 45 minutes or 90?
  - » How often do your classes meet?
  - » Will students need to work outside of class or can everything be accomplished in class time?
- Scheduling requirements
  - » When are your holidays? What is your school year (Aug – June or Jan – Dec)?
  - » Do you want common due dates and times, or flexible dates?
  - » Will students be required to complete specific tasks for their collaborative partners by a certain class lesson?
- Task breakdown for teachers
  - » Who is responsible for what?
  - » When do your tasks need to be completed?
  - » Who will be relying on you to finish your work?
- Technological Requirements
  - » What kinds of technology are needed to complete this project?
  - » What access do teachers and students have? Are you 1:1 or do you have 1 computer per classroom?
  - » What kinds of peripherals will students want to use? How can you leverage the materials you have to benefit all students (perhaps splitting the work so that the school with more access to peripherals completes different tasks)?
- Communication needs
  - » Will students need to communicate in real time at any point?
  - » Do your locations enable you to achieve that during the school day? What is the time difference between your time zones?
  - » If you can't connect real-time, what are the expectations for communication? Daily? Weekly?

Develop a Communication Structure:

It makes sense to have one common "home base" for your project, whether it be a wiki, or a Ning, or a blog – one space where all students and teachers will go to connect with their global partners, one place to store all assignment requirements, one place for all announcement and news, one place for all student artifacts. Items to consider when choosing your "home base":

- Protection level
  - » Does this space need to be private, protected, or public – this has implications for student safety and parent notification
- Tools needed
  - » What kind of things do you want students to be doing?
  - » Does this project require discussion forums, or is threaded discussion by page more appropriate?
  - » Are you looking for a tool that supports media uploading, or are you planning to host your media somewhere else?
  - » Do you want your students to have a space that is "theirs" or do you need to keep the focus on something specific?

Determine Assessment Methods

When students are working collaboratively across great distances, it is especially important to clarify, explicitly, at the beginning of the project, how students will be assessed, including specific assessment tools. Take time to:

- Develop criteria and rubrics
- Be sure to post completed assessment tools on your "home base" so that all students and teachers have access to them.
- Clarify the process of how students will complete the project
- What stages or steps must they go through to complete their project?
- Are parts of the project going be outsourced to different schools based on their resources, location, or experience? How will this be coordinated?

Design Matters:

A good rule of thumb to keep in mind when completing a globally collaborative project is that other teachers may want to look to your completed work as an example, therefore it is essential that your page layout, navigation, and materials are as complete as possible, and easy to understand – even for non-participants. You might want to think of the "home base" as a complete artifact for the entire project – teacher planning, assessment tools, communication strategies, student works, and feedback – so that your "home base" can be a stand-alone resource for teachers around the world.

Think about:

- Having an "about this project" page describing what your goals are with the project and who is participating.
- Having a "participating schools" page to coordinate the schools and students that will be collaborating.

- Having an "assignments" page to place all assignment requirements.
- Having a "students" page for all students to link to their personal online environments.
- Having a "contact us" page to give teachers, students and parents a way to contact you for further information.

To give you an idea of the value of these kinds of collaborations, here are some reflective blog posts (plus many more on our digital content resource page) that we've written over the years:

- Podcasting Power
- A New Year of Collaborations
- The Grade 5 Flat Classroom Experience
- Collaboration Idea Number 3: Creating a Flat Classroom
- Developing the Global Student
- Why Go Global? Or Learning for the Future!
- Ms. Pana (Pana Asavavatana): Kindergarten, Taipei American School, Taiwan

Remember, it's all about the learning!

Most importantly, focus on the learning first. Before starting any of these ideas, ask yourself what do you want students to know and be able to do at the end of this unit, collaboration or experience. You can do all of these types of projects, and provide many different types of learning experiences for your students, no matter which tool you use. The most important part is to focus on the learning outcomes first and then select the tool which best fits the task.

This is the QR Code to access any content that is in blue type & underlined.

It will direct you to a page on our edurolearning.com website that is password-protected.

To access the content, use the password: **Edur0ycc**

8 HELPING PARENTS UNDERSTAND YOUR CONNECTED CLASSROOM

Parent support and engagement in your connected classroom is a key component for success. As excited as you may be about the new and engaging avenues you have discovered for student learning, it's likely that parents may have questions or concerns, and it's important to understand, validate and address those as you help parents understand your connected classroom. Ensuring that parents feel both understood in their concerns and reassured that their children will be safe (and learning) in this new environment will go a long way towards gathering their support.

We highly recommend informing parents as early as possible (soon after you've informed your administrator), and using (or adapting) the documentation we shared in Chapter 3 to ensure that you have parental permission for your students to be participating. Once you've gotten the paperwork out of the way, it's time to share with parents the amazing opportunities you're providing for your students.

Here is our three-step process for successfully helping parents understand your connected classroom.

Step 1: Understanding Parent Concerns

One of the things we know that parents struggle with is the idea that learning looks different today. The problem is, we've all been through school. Many of us are quite successful. So, if that schooling experience worked for us, then it should work for our kids too, right? Not so much. The thing is, learning looks different today, because society is different today. Our job as educators is to ensure that our learning environment reflects reality, not the adult recollection of what school should be. As John Dewey so eloquently said, "If we teach today as we taught yesterday, we rob our children of tomorrow."

As you address parent concerns, you may want to highlight the following:

Learning Purpose for Technology

Of course, this doesn't meant that we should use technology for technology's sake. It's important for parents to know that any technology used in the classroom has an authentic, purposeful reason behind it. Be open with parents about how your students will be using technology to learn. You can use examples of lessons that you'll be teaching, and what students will learn. For example, if you're having your students write blog posts, they will not only be improving their writing skills, they'll be learning important digital citizenship skills.

Safe Use of Technology Combined with Digital Citizenship Skills

It's common for parents to be concerned about their child's online safety. You'll likely get a variety of questions about how you will keep your students safe online. Take this time to explain all of the critical digital citizenship skills you are including as you use technology for learning. Help parents understand that this kind of learning experience builds safe, responsible and respectful online habits and behavior that can be applied in a school setting (where there might already be filters or blocked websites in place) AND outside of school (like a friend's house or a coffee shop, where there might not be any filters at all). It's also worth sharing the strategies you will use to develop class guidelines for appropriate behavior in this context - this is something parents may want to parallel at home.

Curriculum Drives Technology

Keeping the academic focus of your unit at the forefront of your conversation is a great way to demonstrate to parents that your priority is on the learning - not the technology. When learning about all the new tools that you are using with your students, parents may assume that their children are learning technology - not your content area. They may ask things like "what about the math?" or "how will they learn English skills?" It's important to highlight that the technology is being used to enhance or transform learning - not to change the content students are learning. Assuring parents that the focus is still on academic skills helps calm these kinds of concerns.

The Value of Balance

Although we are so excited about the use of technology in the classroom, we are also active proponents of a balanced lifestyle. Just because we are going to be reading online, doesn't mean we stop reading books. Just because we are making connections with other learners around the globe, doesn't mean we stop talking to each other. These concepts may seem obvious to you, but these are frequent (and legitimate) parent concerns. Raising these points right away will help parents understand that you're not "throwing the baby out with the bath water".

Step 2: Educating Parents: Key Talking Points

It can be intimidating talking to parents about something you've just started to explore. So here are six of our most essential talking points that we regularly use with parents. Feel free to adapt them to your needs; these are just starting points to get the conversation going!

1. Learning Looks Different Today.

There is lots of research demonstrating that the skills needed for tomorrow's workforce are different, including The Institute for the Future: 2020 Future Work Skills and the World Economic Forum 10 Skills You Need to Thrive in the Fourth Industrial Revolution. So, if the skills we need to be successful are different, that means that the learning experience should be different too.

2. It's not about content. It's about understanding.

When we went to school, it was all about how much content we could memorize and restate back to the teacher on a test. Sometimes we got lucky and were able to make a poster or a diorama. But other than that, it was all about the content for the test, and not so much about making sense and understanding that content within a wider context.

Today's learning is about demonstrating understanding. Facts are at our fingertips, they're only just a Google away. But understanding what those facts mean, making connections to today's world, to previous learning, and to other subject areas – those skills are far more valuable than factual recall.

3. Learning is Always On

Having access to technology (particularly the internet) means learning doesn't have to stop when we leave the classroom. Students are pursuing independent interests outside school through all sorts of digital means, especially YouTube. Access to the internet means they can learn whatever they want to learn, whenever they want. They can get content that exactly at the right level for their skills, knowledge and understanding, and progress at their own pace. And they can do it whenever they want, about whatever they want. This is individualized learning.

Schools are tapping into that power by providing a 1:1 program (where schools provide, or require, each student to bring a laptop), and enabling and expecting teachers to create a blended learning environment, which means teaching and learning happens both within the classroom environment and online, through the use of all sorts of different tools, the current popular tool is Google Classroom (but there have been plenty of others in the past, and there will be more in the future). A blended classroom model, especially when combined with a 1:1 program, means that learning is accessible anytime, anywhere.

4. It's About Creating, Not Consuming

Technology provides so many new and innovative ways to demonstrate learning – from interactive videos, to long form writing, to interactive representations of complicated data – that learning today is not about how much you can consume, but what you can create with the knowledge and understanding you have developed.

Instead of demonstrating knowledge by taking tests, schools and teachers are developing new and unique ways for students to demonstrate their understanding using media-rich tools, like video, games and even social media. Students are building biomes in Minecraft, participating in ongoing Twitter debates as historical figures, creating collaborative videos with their classmates, and writing books with collaborative partners in another country for release online (in Kindergarten!).

Having access to high powered devices, and the internet, allows students to create authentic products that real-world professionals would create, and then share them with an audience beyond the classroom (more on that in a minute) rather than just filling out worksheets, tests or writing an essay that only the teacher will read.

5. Sharing is BIG

Whether or not we like it, sharing is in. From Instagramming your lunch to maintaining a Snapchat streak with a friend, almost all teens today are sharing their lives in one form or another. And they're expecting (and building) an authentic audience for what they share. It's not enough to just produce content for your teacher (or your classmates) anymore (if it ever was). The goal is to produce something of value for an authentic audience who will actually appreciate that product.

The reality is, as much as teachers like having students create new and unique products to demonstrate their learning, the most important part is having a purpose to the learning. Having a clear understanding of why they are learning, and who they will be demonstrating their learning to, is not only motivational and empowering, but it provides a clear value for the time and energy they spend in both the learning and content production.

6. Interaction and Community are Key

Along with all of this sharing that is quickly becoming part of our culture, and expected as the norm, is the importance of community in the digital space. When we (students and teachers alike) are learning in online spaces, we are becoming part of a community of learners – from women interested in lifting heavy weight to being a first-time home-owner with lots of renovations, we're finding digital spaces that support us in our learning needs, and they are filled with people who want to interact and learn together.

We are able to learn from experts in the field by following them on Instagram, Facebook and Snapchat, and in those spaces, we're able to comment and ask questions – and we expect a response. There's a culture of personal, peer-to-peer connections and conversations that is building in digital spaces. And it's this interaction, this feeling of community, that helps us feel like we're on a learning journey together, even though it's self-directed and individualized for each person involved.

Building this feeling of community in the physical classroom space is not new, for sure, but building that feeling in digital spaces is, and it's more important than ever.

Step 3: Sharing Your Excitement

Once you have all of the academic elements out of the way, we highly recommend that you share your enthusiasm about this experience with the parents of your students. While everything may not go 100% to plan each lesson, your students will be learning valuable skills that will help them throughout their school years and beyond! This attitude of excitement will transfer to your students and to their parents.

You can keep parents engaged in the learning process by inviting them to subscribe to your class blog, or follow your class Twitter or Instagram account. Add in fun and easy "homework" assignments where students are asked to share some of their learning with their parents, and then have parents comment on what they see. Taking simple, but formal, opportunities to have students talk to their parents about their learning (with the visible documentation from your connected classroom) is a great way to keep parents engaged, and help them understand the value of these types of learning experiences.

Remember to be confident when discussing your connected classroom with parents. The connected classroom may be a new concept for parents, so being confident when explaining the types of technology that may be used and how much their child will learn from having access to tech will help them be more confident in the change in learning style.

Step 4: Extra Support

If you're finding that the parents in your classroom (or just one or two) simply need some extra support, you may want to offering them our Parenting in the Digital Age course. This series of courses highlights all of the key elements we talk about with parents when we facilitate face-to-face training sessions - plus each course features a video interview with a parent sharing their tips for navigating the digital world with their children. If parents chose to purchase the six courses as a set, they'll also receive our e-book Top 5 Concerns for Parents in a Digital World for free! If they just want to try something small, they can buy the ebook separately. By joining our newsletter, they will get a free bonus chapter of the eBook too!

Additional Resources

Top 5 Concerns from Parents

- Staying safe online - who are they talking to?
- What aren't they learning at school? What happened to Handwriting and Spelling
- Over-exposed!
- Is my child really learning when playing games online?
- How much screen time is too much time?

Extra Resources

- Partnering with Parents (video)

This is the QR Code to access any content that is in blue type & underlined.

It will direct you to a page on our edurolearning.com website that is password-protected.

To access the content, use the password: **Edur0ycc**

9 CONTINUING THE LEARNING

And there you have it! All of our favorite ideas, tips, strategies and steps for connecting yourself and your students to the world! We hope that this book has provided a strong foundation for you to to get started! Before we wrap up, we would like to take a moment to highlight some of the key takeaways that we hope we have highlighted for you.

Connected Learning is Authentic & Purposeful

As you are testing out new and innovative learning ideas in your classroom, we encourage you to keep SAMR and TPACK in mind so that you are using technology in authentic and purposeful ways. It's exciting to get caught up in the enthusiasm of new tools, but we want to make sure your learning journey with technology is about the pedagogy first, so that you can allow the tools to support, enhance and transform learning experiences.

A PLN is Powerful

Although we have been engaged in our Personal Learning Networks for well over 10 years now, we are still regularly surprised and amazed at the connections we are building for ourselves and for others. We highly encourage you to take the leap and give this a try. Don't feel pressure to have a huge PLN in days, weeks or even months, it takes time and that's all part of the learning journey. We promise that the time invested in building a robust PLN will pay off big time over the long haul. Start small and see where you go!

A Connected Classroom is About People

No matter how you start, whether it's connecting your students to each other within the same classroom, or within your school, or beyond, a connected classroom is all about people. In a world where we are constantly bombarded with the news that technology is isolating us (and in particular young people), let's find the ways that we can use these tools to bring us together - and just as importantly let's demonstrate that to our students, their parents, and our colleagues within our schools.

Connecting Doesn't Mean Distraction

We know it seems overwhelming at first to have all those devices in student hands, but when you transfer all of the skills you already have in terms of classroom management to digital spaces, you can see that you already know how to keep your students focused - even with digital tools at their fingertips. Although you may start using some of our strategies and tips, you'll develop your own unique classroom management strategies over the years. Please share them with us, and with your PLN. There are always teachers new to a connected classroom, and we can all benefit from strategies that work!

Making Time to Create

We love technology, and we hope you do too! But that doesn't mean that we use tech for tech's sake - and it also doesn't mean that we are desperate to "techify" everything. When we take advantage of any version of project-based learning, we can see how technology can be used to empower students in authentic learning experiences that are purposeful, and allow them to share their learning with a real-world audience. As you bring more technology into your classroom, remember to structure those learning experiences with the design cycle process in mind so that your students prosumers - we want them to be creators of content, along with being consumers.

Bring the World to Your Classroom

We are inspired by the endless opportunities that technology can bring to our classrooms. And, in particular, as teachers who have lived and worked in a variety of countries, the opportunity to connect, explore, understand and empathize with people all around the world, we value the ease with which you can bring the world into your classroom.

As you start to connect your students to each other, and yourself to a wider PLN, keep your eyes open for opportunities for your students to better understand the diverse world we live in. You might be surprised at the connections you can make, and how easily you can bring outside experience and expertise into your classroom. Technology is going to continue to open up more of the world to us, ensuring that our students are ready for this interconnected world, able to communicate and collaborate across cultures and time zones is already a critical skill that will only become more and more valuable

Parents Are Our Partners

One of the biggest lessons we have learned as technology advocates in schools is how powerful parents can be, as our partners in learning. We know that parents only want the best for their children. Ensuring that we take the time to involve, engage and educate them in the value that technology has to offer means that they will not only be able to support their children, but they will also be able to support you in your efforts to innovate your classroom.

Learn More With Eduro Learning

When you're ready to learn more, we invite you to visit our website for additional books, online courses, year-long micro-credentials, and face-to-face events. Follow us on social media to stay connected with all the great resources we share. And let us know how you're applying your key learnings from this book! We love to share teacher stories on our blog and we welcome your ideas and input into how we can support you further. We look forward to seeing you - online and off!

This is the QR Code to access any content that is in blue type & underlined.

It will direct you to a page on our edurolearning.com website that is password-protected.

To access the content, use the password:
Edur0ycc

Contact Us

 www.edurolearning.com

 services@edurolearning.com

Connect with Us

 https://facebook.com/edurolearning

  @edurolearning

Made in the USA
Coppell, TX
15 June 2024

33553457R10056